Just a Mum

Legacy of Love

Letters to Our Children

Just A Mum: Legacy of Love. Authors from around the World took the time to tell their children of this world and those passed, exactly what they needed to. Pouring out their hearts and leaving a Legacy of Love from the Ports of Maine USA, crossing into the hearts of the UK. Just a Mum. Legacy of Love.

Warrior and Queen gratefully acknowledge the many incredible individuals who granted Warrior and Queen permission to reprint the cited material.

Front cover photo is courtesy of Stina M. Gray of www.warriorandqueen.com

Just A Mum Legacy of Love
Stina M. Gray
[Editor] Susan J Clegg

★The letters in this book are based on the reality and opinions of the Authors who contributed their individual experiences. They represent one side to a story. Warrior and Queen have done all possible to protect all parties involved with the suggestion of name changes. Warrior and Queen cannot confirm that all the events of these letters are factual.

First Published: May 2021

Contents

13. Chelsea Canonico

14. Vicky Robinson

15. Leigh Barnard

16. Naomi Eskowitz

17. Sami Speakman

18. Nicola Reynolds

19. Sue Clegg

20. Gemma Walkden

21. Mel Broughton

22. Colleen Higgins

23. Hollie Ann

24. Jennifer Williams-Royle

25. Erin James

26. Jade Baxter

27. Stina M. Gray

Afterthought – Stina M. Gray

IN LOVING MEMORY OF

CLARE DURHAM

During the writing of this book, we lost a valued member of our community. We want to honour her the best way we know how, from the heart.

Dear Clare,

As a friend you were the most loyal and beautiful person I have known. I know everyone says that when they lose someone they love, but truly, you were incredible. Such a fierce Mum and a fighter through and through. The Embodiment of Warrior and Queen. Fighting for what your children needed and deserved whilst never complaining. Always turning up with a smile on your face, even when I wanted to scream about the world. You saw the Brightside in everything. You were Sunshine. On the dreariest day. From good food to an adventure, you brought joy to my world.

Your children will grow proud of the woman you were. Proud of all you have instilled in them and proud that their mum never gave up. Right up until the very end. Rightly so, they worshipped you and you adored them. My heart breaks for them, but I promise, your Legacy will live on. Through your friends, your family and the incredible times you gave to us all. I will treasure the comfort that was in your smile and your ability to find a silver lining. I will keep you in memory and heart for a lifetime.

My dearest friend, I miss you, I love you and I see your true colours, time after time. Your sunshine brought a rainbow during my storms and you made sure that my memories are filled with us two girls, who wanted to have fun!

Rest Now Queen.

Love Bex xx

Foreword

A legacy left by will is often measured in money or personal property. We can get lost in the idea that someone, somewhere might leave us a fortune and life would be awesome. It's like that lottery dream we all have, what would I spend it on? Life would be perfect. The reality for many is very different, hardworking people slogging away for a lifetime to leave something of value to their loved ones when their time comes. The Authors in this book know that whilst money is super useful for day-to-day survival, it's also nothing close to the Love they feel for their children. There is no amount of money that could be placed on the Legacy of Love.

Ancestors leave their mark on the world for generations after they have gone. Shaping history with the valuable lessons they left behind, creating the pathway to a valuable future. Did you ever say something and think that you sounded like your Mum? Or your Nan? Or someone who you loved dearly? A Legacy of Love exists in that moment. It's in a recipe you remember from your childhood, a story you were told as you grew older or a song you have always loved singing together. Passing on legacies is something we don't always realise we do. Quite often it's only when somebody loses a person they love, they begin to look into the deep and meaningful of life. Which in itself is a tragedy.

Imagine if we said and did everything we wanted to, with each other in waking life. OK, maybe not ALL the things. There are definitely a few things that are not productive to say out loud, but for the most part, if we spoke about our feelings, our struggles, failings and achievements more often, we might find that the stigma's we battle, lose a little of their power. We might even find that we pass on some healthy habits to future generations.

Imagine a future generation that wasn't afraid to reach out for help. A generation who believed that speaking up about the reality of the world would make a difference. A generation fuelled with love and acceptance for who they truly are. A Generation of Love. What a beautiful Legacy that would be.

Every moment you spend with your child is part of your legacy. Every moment you spend making your life better is part of your legacy. Every self-development skill, every hour of overtime or every meal prepared with love (even the rushed McDonalds trip between afterschool clubs!) It all counts. Everything you do today, shapes tomorrow. Take time to feed your soul so that its fruits are passed on for years to come. To encourage wanderlust and all of the amazing benefits of exploration.

There is no need to grow an empire or discover something new to be able to leave a legacy. It's in your words. Your hugs. Your homemade meatballs and Sunday night family movies. Every single one of you reading this book has the power to change the world. For at very least one person. Be that yourself or your offspring. The magic is in your interactions. Conjure happiness and love. Peace for your full life whilst chasing rainbows and dancing through storms. How you do things moving forward is the most important bit. Yesterday has happened. Sadly, we can't change any of that. All we can do is learn from it and continue on, honouring the legacy of those gone before us. Honouring ourselves and those yet to follow.

The Authors in this book have delved deep into their emotions and wrote letters from the heart. Letters that they never realised they needed to write. Letters to the most important people in the world. It's not an easy task. The benefit however, far outweighs the pain. Writing in this way helps heal the past, it reassures the present and it contributes towards the future. It immortalises the wishes of the most incredible people to walk the earth. Mothers.

Pretty sure that's better than a 3 bed semi full of doilies and blue china!

Enjoy!

Stina xx

1.

Lindsey Appleton

To My 2 Little Girls - You Are My World

Dear Baby Girl #1, from the age of 4 weeks old our life as a family was turned upside down by domestic violence.

The day your dad laid his hands on me was the first and last time I would ever let that happen.

I moved us away for a fresh start to be near your nana, grandad and 2 uncles who all love you very much.

In 2018 you were diagnosed with Autism and I never stopped fighting for you, to see all the specialists needed to get you the correct support at school to help you emotionally and academically.

I will never stop fighting for you, I love you so so much and I'm so proud of how far you have come in the short amount of time you have been in this crazy world.

I love you xx

Dear Baby Girl #2, I'm so sorry you never got to know what it felt like to have a family where a mum & dad were together from the moment you arrived into this crazy world.

Being pregnant with you spurred me on to proving to myself that I was able to do this and become a better version of myself and a better parent for both you and your sister.

Your dad chose to leave before you were born, with him and his whole family turning their back on us until after you were born, conveniently for them not having to help out and get things ready for your arrival. That is a reflection of them and the kind of people they are.

Your family right here will never turn their back on you.

At 36 weeks pregnant I enrolled on a teaching course and never looked back. You were my inspiration and my drive – I wanted to succeed and do this for us, for our little family!

Bettering myself for you girls, to give you a better life.

Showing you that mummy can do this single handedly.

Hell I brought you into this world with your dad nowhere to be seen.

This is all I've ever known and I'm doing what I can to the best of my ability, putting my all into it every day for you girls.

You fought to be here after being rushed to intensive care from birth, I never left your side.

You are my warrior, my little inspiration.

Now mummy is warrioring on single handedly for my two little princesses.

I love you so much my brave little fighter xx

2.

Mahmuda Hill

Inspired By Love

So much has changed since I wrote this speech for my eldest daughter's 18th birthday. These were my thoughts 5 years ago...

"I was told that it was highly unlikely I would ever get pregnant, how wrong they were!!! I found out I was pregnant very early on, 7 weeks, and you were a miracle, the first of four. I had to have an emergency scan and from the moment we saw you, yes you were just a blob, we loved you. As first-time parents we had no idea what to expect. You caused my liver to malfunction and I was covered in a horrible rash but I was happy. That was nothing compared to the moment you were born and the feeling of utter happiness and unconditional love for you.

You were a clingy and yes whiney baby, but adorable. When you became a big sister for the first time you shone at the role. And with each sibling you showed more willingness to help and care for them.

When your dad was killed you were a tender age of 9, you stepped into an adult role in the care of your baby brother, changing his nappies, and helping your sisters with everything Daddy used to do. And so much more by taking care of me too. I can honestly say the first 2 and a half years afterwards I can't remember, I missed so much of all of you developing and growing during this time. You held us together, my little trouper. As you grew older you started to take over the cooking and have excelled in this too. You are a born protector and care giver. Daddy would be so proud of you.

As the years have passed you have struggled with not having your Dad here, we have all struggled, but I know without a shadow of a doubt that he would be proud of the young lady standing in front of us. He may not be here physically, but he is here in us all, in our hearts and thoughts and in all 4 of you. He would be proud of you all and would love you all as much as I do. He is alive in us and always watching over us.

As a parent I don't get it right every time and you might even think I never get it right, but I can say, with my hand on my heart, that you four are the best of us, a credit to both me and your daddy. I wish I could take the pain away of the loss of Daddy, but I can't, just know he would be here if he could.

You're 18 now and half your life has been without Daddy, just remember how much he loved you and always will, that love can never die. I am and will always be here for all of you and will support you in whatever path you choose. All I can wish for you, everything I prayer for you, is that you are happy and find a true love like I did with daddy.

I would like everyone to join me in wishing my daughter a happy birthday and may you succeed in all that you do with a happiness in your heart always and forever."

I was unable to read this speech at the time, and my friend had to take over, there wasn't a dry eye in the room.

Every year on Daddy's death anniversary you kept saying you felt guilty about his death, but you couldn't or wouldn't explain why you felt like this. I knew why, I always knew, but it wasn't what I believed to be true, and I needed you to tell me why in your own words. Eventually, on the 10th anniversary you told me why…

Every Monday Daddy used to come home early to take you to Guides, but that fateful day Guides had been cancelled. In the mind of a 9-year-old, that was the reason Daddy died in a car accident. IF ONLY Guides was on, he would have left work on time. IF ONLY he left on time, he wouldn't have been hit by that other car!!

I have NEVER thought this, but I knew this was what was going on in your mind. I was scared to put the thought into voice just in case you thought I blamed you!! It was NOT your fault my beautiful girl. It was JUST his time, preordained by God.

I thought I was doing the right thing, I thought that the fact I always said it was his time to die, and that the other driver was just a kid that made a mistake, was enough. The fact that I said I didn't want any of us to hate the other driver because I didn't want that blackness and hatred to engulf us. The fact that I brought you up to be kind and generous and to see how blessed we are. The fact we have had amazing holidays, because I didn't want Daddy's death to be the only childhood memory, I wanted you to have happy memories. I thought it would be enough, I was wrong, and I'm sorry for that.

All of you have suffered and still suffering so much, it breaks my heart to know that I can't take your pain away.

On my middle daughter's 18th birthday, we spent the day at my dad's bed watching him die, I think he waited till after midnight, so it wasn't her birthday anymore. The scream she let out as Nana took his last breath, I had to push family out of the way to get to her, and you took over again. You messaged everyone that needed to know, and then you sat with her and held her as I tried to comfort your Nanu, my mum. You took her home and woke up your siblings to tell them the news.

But I didn't see how it affected you, you spiralled, and I didn't notice, I was too preoccupied with sorting the funeral. Your sister was helping me, and I was grateful for that but couldn't understand why you had distanced yourself from me. We were always so close. And I'm sorry for that.

It didn't take me long to notice, but a month is still too long, and I insisted I go with you to the doctors. He asked if you were suicidal, you said no you would never do that. But I said he didn't ask if you would do it, he asked if you felt like it. And that's when he asked about the self-harming!! I didn't know, I'm your mum and I should have known.

I'm so sorry I failed you and let you down.

Once I knew, we were able to talk about the reason, I wasn't going to let this be another 10 years of your life like when Daddy died. AGAIN, guilt reared its ugly head. You felt guilty for not being upset that Nana had died!! But I told you I wasn't upset he had died, I was upset he hadn't been able to be the grandfather you needed after your Daddy's death. It wasn't his fault that he had dementia, it wasn't his fault he was in a nursing home for the last 7 years of his life, bed ridden. I was glad, if that's the right way to put it, that he had died, because he didn't have any quality of life. He was in a better place now. That conversation needed to happen, as hard as it was.

It didn't stop you having the feelings or even stop you completely, but you knew you could talk to me which helped. The last time, was just before my 50th birthday, you wanted to make my birthday perfect just like Daddy would have. That pressure was too much for you. But all I have ever wanted was for you all to be happy and that is the best present for me.

We have come a long way then. So many ups and downs for us all. Nana's death was hardest for your younger sister, she was sitting A levels at the time and wouldn't go back to school. She had been so strong leading up to the funeral, at my side constantly helping me with all the paperwork. You managed to get her to go into school so she could sit her exams. She got amazing results, but she wasn't happy and wanted to resit them. But you helped her see that her results were good enough for her to go to her university of choice doing the course she wanted.

I am so proud of you all and know Daddy would be so proud too.

And now we are in the midst of a worldwide pandemic, and your youngest sister had her A level results totally messed up due to the criteria used for grading!! She is resitting and will prove everyone wrong I'm sure. Her expected results were As and Bs and they gave her all Cs (after initially giving her Ds)! The criteria used 1) wrong postcode 2) single parent family (I'm not single I'm a Widow) 3) ethnic minority!!! Screwed on all accounts, nothing to do with how capable she was as an individual!

Your baby brother is struggling with the pandemic, and this year he should be doing his GCSEs, I have resigned myself to this academic year being a right off for him! His mental health is more important than any grade.

But we also celebrated your Islamic Wedding and seeing you all smiling and laughing is what makes my heart feel warm and happy. The night of your wedding I dreamt of your Daddy, he looked so happy, the perfect end to a perfect day. I wish you both all the happiness in the world, a blessed and happy marriage full of love always.

I may not have been the perfect parent, I have lost my temper, I have not always understood how you all feel, but I have and will always love you, as does Daddy.

All my love today and forever,

Mummy

3.

Lucy Diep

To The Loves of My Life, Josh, Connor & Esmee

Firstly, I wanted to say how much I love you all. You are all amazing children, and I wouldn't change you for the world. You three are what kept me going in my dark times. You are what give me purpose and you are all my biggest accomplishments. I am so proud of you all and the people you have become and are turning into.

It's 2021 and right now the world is a pretty crazy place, the world is full of mask and non-mask wearers, the people fearing Covid and the conspiracy theorists. Everyone's worried whether they should have the vaccine or whether it will alter the human body and we all become zombies or robots. The vaccine was created so fast and hasn't had much time to be tested so I am very wary right now on whether this is safe or not. I guess time will tell. So many conspiracies are out there some crazy, some not so crazy. You are old enough to know what you want to believe but don't believe something just because you are told it. Question everything, make your own mind up.

You are not allowed to attend school or go out to meet your friends because it is no longer safe. Schooling is done online, and people are out fighting over toilet roll and pasta. You are only allowed to shop for essentials or medicine. I wish I could change the world you live in and the craziness and hurting that we come across daily, it's so scary and worrying. I want to protect you, but how do I protect you from something that can't be seen, that is new and I don't know a lot about. It made me wonder what would happen if I was no longer here, which is why I write this letter, in the event that I am no longer around. I wanted to leave behind something for you to know how much I love you all.

Joshua
You are my firstborn; I was only young when I had you but it gave us a unique bond of friendship as well as mother and son. I would not change how young I was because if I had waited you wouldn't be who you are today. From the day I found out I was pregnant with you my life changed for the better. Yes, some times were scary and worrying but you all made life so worthwhile.

I know one day you are going to be a great father; you are amazing with children. You have a very smart mind, and you are very clever, you just need to put it to good use. You always treat people with respect and kindness, and I love that about you. You always put family first and that's exactly how it should be. I am very proud of the man you have become. I know you struggle to cope with day-to-day normality and escape into your own world and I hope one day that you are in a happier place, where you can enjoy life as you should be, as you deserve to be. I want you to be the glue that holds all three of you together. At the end of the day, you have known me the longest and know exactly how my mind works and how I would do things. Connor and Esmee struggle to cope with the emotions and how they deal with the world, I want you to guide them and keep them on the straight and narrow but also enjoy being the oldest brother. Enjoy your time with them and remember you are their friend as well as their brother.

Connor
You are such a lovely boy; you are kind and loving and everyone who meets you says how caring you are. I know you struggle with learning, but I am

proud of how far you have come since high school, your achievements of sticking with college and circus. Hopefully these qualities will help you in the future to get where you want to in life.

I know sometimes you struggle with confidence but you have got this! Stick at it and ask for help if you need it. I have every faith in you. Never be too proud to ask something if you don't know how to do something or the answer to something.

Dyspraxia and dyslexia have been a struggle for you and a big part of your life but you haven't let it hold you back so don't start now. Keep trying and you will go far. Look after your baby sister and older brother. You and Josh were close once, it would be nice for you to be like that again. Esmee also has learning difficulties and will need your help and guidance on how to cope. Keep being yourself and let yourself shine.

When things don't go your way and times get hard don't give up. Things can get better. Remember when you were in very dark times, all the changes we made to help build you back up. You can do it again it's never too late to try again.

Esmee

My baby girl, you are so beautiful and amazing. I know right now you are non-verbal and you struggle communicating with your family and at nursery but you will get there. We are in the process of getting you the help you need so the world can hear your voice and see how amazing you are. Your elder brothers will always be around to look after you and keep away those annoying boys in the future.

I love how loving you are. You give the best cuddles and have such an amazing smile. Mummy loves you very much and I am sure you are going to grow up to be a very nice, kind, caring person. I enjoy our fun times dancing in the kitchen and just being silly.

Never let anyone make you feel you are not good enough. If anyone tries to pick on you for being different it is a reflection on what a horrible person they are. You are amazing and never let anyone tell you any different.

I would love for you to find something that you enjoy doing and enroll in a class. Connor did circus and that helped him a lot and I think something like that would be really good fun and help you to grow and also make friends.

Some friends come and go but you will always have family and friends, and people watching out for you and wanting the best for you. Your dad and your brothers will always be there no matter what obstacles come your way and I will be beside you, holding your hand.

Whatever happens I want you all to stick together I want you all to grow up around each other and always be in each other's lives. I want you to always make time for each other and always check up on each other. I know it will be hard without me but please never give up on life. You know how much it affected me when Lindsay left and I wouldn't want any of you to leave the world that way. Suicide does not make other people's lives better. I know you have seen how much I have struggled with Lindsay not being here and I hope that makes you realise that suicide isn't the end of the story for those left behind.

My biggest hope for you is that you are happy in whatever you are doing. You are loved so much and I want you to be each other's rock. At Christmas and special occasions I want you all to get together and spend the day together if possible.

Spoil your loved ones when you can but don't make my mistake by getting into debt. Debt was a big problem for me because I wanted to give you all everything you deserved even if I didn't have the money to do so. I hope your childhood was a good childhood. I tried to give you all the love, support and fun that I could. I tried to get you the things that you wanted and give you Christmases and birthdays that I never had. I tried my best.

I love you all so much and I will always be looking over you, sending you love. When you are sad and upset I will be by your side giving you a big cuddle.

All my love
mum
xxx

4.

Shammy Walton

What Happened To Daddy

Dearest Maya,

I am writing this letter because I want to tell you about the last few months I had with your Dad.

He was the love of my life.

Your father and I used to talk about losing our parents. I lost my Mum aged 3, she was on life support for 6 months. Your Dad lost his father, age 12. They were both horrific deaths. We used to sit and talk about how sometimes we couldn't picture their faces or remember their voices.

Your Dad and I had this in common. Neither of us had the best childhood and we knew before we had you, we were going to give you the happiest life.

We were both pretty wild when we got together. We had known each other a very long time. I met him when he was 12. I was best friends with his cousin.

Many times, I partied with him never knowing he would be the one for me.

I'd not seen him for some time. I was 35, he was 27. I remember the day when I looked in his eyes and I thought instantly you're the one. I'm going to have your child. I knew, in that moment...

We were so deeply in love. It was the best feeling I've ever had. He made me so happy. Every Friday he would buy me flowers and every morning I would get up and make his breakfast before he went to work. Sometimes I would get up at 5.45 am. I have never done that for anyone before and safe to say I will never do it again.

The next 7 years were the happiest of my life.

You were our rainbow baby, we miscarried before you. I always felt she was a girl, 11 weeks and 5 days and there was no heartbeat. Your Dad and I were so sad. Not long afterwards I was pregnant with you. We were overjoyed. We wanted you so much. I knew your name before you were conceived.

The next few years were so happy. I loved your Dad so much; he was my best friend. I miss him more than my words can express. He was absolutely my soulmate, and we had the type of love everyone longs for, but some never experience.

Then on your 4th birthday I will never ever forget. Your Dad had been feeling unwell. The day before he was at your birthday party with all of us. But he was so unwell. His skin had become yellow, and he had lost so much weight. I saw him wobble to sit down and my heart dropped.

He wouldn't go to the doctors but the following day I made him. The doctor could tell from an ultrasound scan that he had cancer. I will never forget those words. Your Dad was so upset he couldn't tell me himself he had the doctor speak to me on the phone.

We later found out he had cholangiocarcinoma. It's a very rare liver cancer. It was inoperable.

He asked the lady at the hospital, "Can't I just have a new liver. Alcoholics get liver transplants all the time?". "No Sean" she said, "In this type of case it will keep coming back".

I've never seen your Dad breakdown like he did that day. We were both in shock, and from that day I knew he was dying. Every time I looked into his beautiful, big, blue eyes; I stared a little longer so I could cherish it. Every time I held him; I sniffed a little longer so I could put that smell in my memory box in my head.

I got him on a vegan diet, but you remember how he loved spam and burgers. He loved eating shit food. His idea of a romantic meal with me was a McDonald's breakfast in bed. He put up with my food for around 3 weeks. I laced it with cannabis to help with the pain.

We were in the hospital awaiting results from another scan and he reminded me I hadn't eaten. He told me to share what I had made. I was starving, so I did.

By the time the doctor came to talk to us I was off my face. I could see the doctor's lips move but not much was going in. Your Dad and I were laughing even though it was such a serious moment.

Not long after this he was admitted into the hospital, I had to call an ambulance and he never came home. By this point I had given up on the vegan thing and he ate what he wanted. His diet consisted of Uncle Skinner's bacon butties, McDonald's and generally shit food. But who was I to tell him he couldn't eat it. He was a dying man.

He became so skeletal it scared the hell out of me, but I continued to show him love, support and positivity. He had gone from a strong scaffolder, who was super fit, to an old man in a matter of weeks. I can't tell you how hard this was to watch. He is still the strongest man I ever met, and he was still so polite to all the people who looked after him.

He was lying in his bed and every inch of his body was giving him pain. He asked me to climb on the bed for a cuddle, I knew it was hurting him, but we both knew it would be the last time we snuggled.

I gave him reiki daily, always with my hands on him. He used to call me bat shit crazy, but at this point he loved and needed it.

One day there was an issue with a stent he'd had fitted and he developed pancreatitis. He was so ill. It was September 4th. I thought he was going to die. I knew I had to marry him there and then. With the help of our beautiful friends we did. We were married in his hospital room. It was the happiest and saddest day of my life.

Our wedding night was spent with a bottle of pink gin and the lovely sister on the ward let your Dad smoke a joint or three in his room. We laughed and chatted all night. It was one of the best nights of my life. I was so happy, but I knew what was coming.

In the weeks following I was giving your Dad cannabis oil. Up his bum, in his mouth, in every way I could. For a man who loved the weed I think he got to the point where he hated it. Some days he seemed fine but then he would sleep for two. As this began to happen more frequently, I knew I had to say my goodbyes.

In the beginning of his stay in hospital, my routine was, drop you at school, go straight to the hospital. I would then leave your Dad and pick you up at 3, bring you home, cook your dinner and bath you, read your story and get you in bed. The minute you closed your eyes I would wait for our sitter and get back to the hospital. Our friends took it in turns to sit in the house every night. Sometimes I wouldn't get back till 6 or 7 in the morning, but I always made sure I took you to school.

I don't know where I got my strength from, but my love for you is what kept me going through all of this. I tried to keep your life as 'normal' as possible.

I remember when my mum died, I didn't really see my Dad. It was tough so I made sure I gave you the love and care you needed, no matter how hard it was.

After a while I had to tell your Dad I couldn't continue to sleep at the hospital because I was exhausted. But that was a lie, I knew in my heart the next time I stayed he would die. So, I put it off as long as I could and started coming home before midnight.

Your father told me he couldn't take the pain anymore and he wanted to go. I told him it was ok, and I didn't want him in pain either. He asked my permission to give up and I told him it was fine. I told him we would be together again one day. He told me he didn't believe in that shit. Safe to say I think he does now angel.

I took you to hospital for the last time. He held you and sobbed like a baby. I knew this would be the last time you would see each other.

That Friday I went to the hospital to stay over. I took a bottle of pink gin and lemonade. I sat with him but he could not speak. I knew it was time. I placed my hand on his heart and lay as close to him as I could. Around 1, maybe 2 am. I felt his heartbeat become so faint until it stopped. I told him I loved him and I would look after you.

You are a constant reminder to me of your Dad, sometimes this makes me so happy other times it makes me feel so sad.

I'm telling you all this now because you were so little when this happened.

You are the best thing that has ever happened to me and you have been my rock through all of this. Without you by my side I could never have looked after your Dad and stayed strong. As much as you need me, I also need you.

Your Father wrote you this letter:

A message to Maya from Daddy

You have given me the proudest 4 years of my life.

Thank you

You can be anything you want to be.

I'm so sorry I can't be there for you. You and your mummy were all I ever wanted.

Be the nicest person you can be.

You're so beautiful, clever and smart and you are the nicest person I have ever met.

You make me happy every day and the first time I touched you I felt so much love and have never been prouder.

I will always be with you in your heart forever.

Love Daddy

We are now in our third lockdown as I write you this letter. Watching the world close down because of Covid has been just as crazy as watching what happened to Dad.

Nothing in life is guaranteed, every moment is a blessing. Take nothing for granted and do not waste a minute.

I want to say, if I seem sad sometimes, I'm so sorry. Your Dad was my best friend, and I was looking forward to spending my life with him. I've felt so many emotions in these lockdowns, anger, sadness, and self-pity to name a few. So, if I have been grumpy with you, I apologise from the bottom of my heart.

I'm sad because I'm heartbroken and being without him is really tough. I always knew it was going to be hard to raise you without having my own mother, but now not having your Dad makes it so much harder. Sometimes it feels like I am running up hill with a bag of rocks on my back. I know it won't always feel like this my angel.

The future for us looks very bright.

I look forward to our future. I have half my life left to spend with you. I can't wait to make new and happy memories together. I'm looking forward to seeing the woman you will become.

I want you to know that we will always have this sadness because we lost Daddy, but you have to know we can still be happy. Being without my own mum really helps me to understand what you are going through.

Life is what you make it and no matter what it throws at you, remember you are a strong woman, and you are from a family of strong humans. You are amazing and you deserve happiness.

Sometimes when bad things happen it's easy to stay angry, but this will only hurt you in the long run. Be kind, don't live with hate or bitterness in your heart. Always forgive and keep love in mind with everything you do. As long as you do everything from a place of love, you will be just fine.

I will also look forward to the day when you don't leave your poos in the toilet.

All my love
Mum xx

Little poem for my Mam.

My parents were immigrants,
And came to Great Britain
They met at Manchester Uni –
I 'd like to think they were smitten.

I'm not very sure though,
because they had a shotgun wedding.
A child out of wedlock,
was not where they were supposed to be heading.

In the very early eighties this would have been so
bad,
It would have made both their 'BAME' families
really sad.

Pause.

So who the fuck says BAME?
Where did this come from?
Wasn't around in the 80s
What a horrible name...

The new style of race hate I guess,
From the Tory government I wouldn't expect
anything less,

Divide the people so you can carry on with your shit
show.
Divide and conquer is the oldest rule in the book,
you know.

Anyway, back to the story of why my parents came
here,
They were so brave because none of their families
were near.

Imagine starting your life in a new country on your
own.
Takes fucking guts and I'm proud of them both.

They came over here for a better life,
Similar to the land of the free and all that shite.
Back then in late 70s and 80s racism was rife,
Being a person of colour, so different to being
white.

When I was a kid, skinheads were national front,
I later realised that not every skinhead was a cunt.

My mum was very political, fought for human
rights.
Always on human rights marches and getting into
fights.

She was a warrior in the true sense of the word.
To her, Inequality was fucking absurd.
Discrimination because of your race or gender,
Really pushed her buttons, it would really offend
her.

So instead of sitting on her arse moaning about it,
She believed she could make a difference and did
something about it!

She would go down to London to fight her cause,
Physically fighting with NF and marching against
illegal wars.

I remember marches in the days of Maggie
Thatcher,
Shouting slogans about the baby milk snatcher!
Everyone called each other comrade and wore
scarves the colour red.
Who knew a couple of years later she would be
dead.

One day she was down London for her work with
human rights,
She was walking on the pavement and got hit by a
motorbike.

Years later I found out the guy was SAS,
What really happened is anyone's guess.

She was on life support for 26 weeks,
I never again heard her speak.
God how I miss her,
But she lives on in me and my daughter.

Last time I saw her she was lying in a bed,

Mad hair everywhere and tubes around her head.
To me she is a hero and I love her madly,
To be so passionate is great - but it ended badly.

5.

Tanya Sparey

To My Smallest Rainbow, You Give Me The Greatest Joy

Dear Chiana,

It's time I shared a few things with you. At the time of writing this you are 1 week shy of your 4th birthday. You are happy and healthy, and every cuddle, giggle, smile and new little personality that you share with me gives me a warm happy feeling inside. You have such a beautiful nature and I want to help ensure you always have the support and lessons you need in life to be your truest and happiest self.

My biggest and most vital lesson is about communication. You are a little chatterbox at the moment and when someone says something you don't like, you know the solution is to 'talk'. This is crucial for all your relationships, whether they are work, family, friends or partners. Shouting is never productive, although feels necessary. Always take every disagreement as an opportunity to work out a solution that works for everyone. And remember it's

OK to have a different opinion, make sure it is a well-informed one, and always listen and accept others will have different points of view.

This leads me nicely on to comparison is a confidence killer. Take inspiration from other people and all of your experiences to help you to discover who you are, how you want to show yourself to the world, what you do in life, and how you see yourself. What you see in the world is very often a perfect moment, you don't always see what happens behind closed doors. No-one needs to understand your journey, as it is your journey. It is nice to have an end to journey towards, but it is the journey that matters in the end.

On your journey through life, you will make mistakes, experience difficulties and challenges. Every single one of these will shape you, make you stronger and make you, more you. You can't have sunshine and rainbows without those clouds, so when you get those rainbows, cover yourself with them, and be the rainbow in other people's clouds. Don't be afraid to make mistakes, never be ashamed of them, learn from every one. **If we were all perfect, we'd be making photographs and we'd be carbon copies of each other. Mistakes are your style, so embrace them.** It sounds like a cliché but you are allowed to be both a masterpiece and a work in progress simultaneously. Failure is success in progress.

Take risks but know the risks before you take them. Understand what the risk to reward payoff is. This is also a lesson that will come up throughout your daily life. It could be about finances, know the risks of debt and stay away from it where you can. Live within your means, and don't get caught up by possessions. Value experiences, enjoy the moments that life has to offer and take the time to enjoy them. Take the time to see what you have as well as who you are surrounded by, no matter how big or small your world is.

Try everything, and don't feel like once you have made a choice you are stuck with it. You won't know what you want to be doing at 30 when you are 15, so do what you enjoy in the moment. It's never too late to take a different path, or even many paths. If you grow up to be anything like me, you will have many, many different passions, and you can do them all. You can do whatever you want to, you can sweep the streets or stack shelves so long as you are happy, safe and within the law. This is something my parents taught me, and a legacy lesson I want to pass to you with love from your grandad and Gano.

Time will always be an excuse for not doing something, make sure you always have balance. Make time for yourself every day, after all you are your longest commitment. Do what you need to do and do what you want to do. You don't have to reach all of your dreams immediately, but a dream that becomes a plan, becomes a reality (even if it changes along the way). Take steps every day towards the life you want to have. Don't look back, you aren't going that way.

Be your most authentic self in the moment. By being you, and doing you, you will attract your tribe. You are the friendliest, most trusting child I know. But be aware that not everyone will be good to have in your life. We will have the 'stranger danger' conversation soon enough. Walk away from toxic relationships. Embrace positive human interactions, surround yourself by supportive people. A brilliant way to really appreciate what you have is to practice mindfulness. Stop and use all your senses to experience the moments. Take 5 minutes to feel, then dust yourself off and get on with your day. I'm so proud that you already know when you are getting worked up, angry or excitable and you need to take a break; you take some deep breaths and a Namaste. Write a journal,

47

even if it is just a few things you are grateful for every day and especially on your worst days. This is a habit I hope to get you into very soon.

Work out what your 'why' is. This can be multi levelled but mine is to be happy and make a positive impact on the people around me and this is all I want for you.

And finally, love, it comes in many forms. But it might be someone putting your socks and shoes on when you can't reach (like your dad, when I was pregnant with you), wafting the smell of a cuppa towards you in the morning to wake you gently or still being best friends and talking about everything, even when you know each other really well. Love is what's in the room on Christmas Day if you stop opening presents and just listen. When you find this love, cherish it and enjoy the moments.

You are so precious to me,

Mum

PS I love you

6.

Fiona Halliday

Be Yourselves

Dear Ellie and Essie,

As I begin to write, you are upstairs getting on with your home-schooling. I hope this time will not be a difficult memory for you. I'm writing to tell you about time before you were born, life with you when you were little, life with you now and my hopes for you in the future.

Ellie, when your dad and I found out we were expecting you we were overjoyed. Literally, you were an answer to prayer. On that day, I saw a rainbow, and, while I know you don't share my beliefs, I remembered that God listened to me. You were a very cute baby (all Mums say that, don't they?). So was your sister! Essie, I've not forgotten you! We wanted your big sister to be a big sister – a sibling is such a great thing – well, maybe you'll see that when you're adults! We were just as thrilled and excited to know we were having you when the time came.

So, I had two beautiful girls and I was incredibly happy. I didn't see that life would change at any time in the near future. You were adored by all the family and all your grandparents took turns to look after you when I was working. Although I didn't go back to work full time; I needed that time to be me. I needed to be able to make a difference outside the home. As you know, I'm not good at keeping the house tidy!

We had some great times in the holidays, and we had terrible times when family members became ill. When we lost your Grampa, life changed immeasurably. I was worried about my Mum, and I lost a compass in my life. Your Dad was amazing and supportive, but he couldn't understand completely how life had changed for me. This was reflected, I think, in my parenting. I didn't read you as many stories as I once had. I watched too much television (still do). I found it difficult to help you in your grief. For a few years, I gave up, just went through the motions. It wasn't obvious to other people; it was inexplicable.

However, I feel that life did turn a corner and I started being able to let my Mum do things without me some of the time (we still speak most days!) and a bit of balance came back.

You two have always been so studious and your teachers think you're lovely. We are proud of how you are growing up.

Being the people that you are is especially important. Don't ever feel that you need to be someone else. You both have talents. Ellie, you are funny and good at writing and you're 'ever so slightly' dramatic. I want to have a front row seat whenever you get an award! Essie, you are a consummate artist, at 12, you can draw and animate and, when you are a famous artist, you'll be able to look after me and your Dad in our old age!

I know life can throw us curve balls; the 2020 pandemic, which is ongoing, is one heck of a curve ball; but you can do whatever you want in life. You can be whoever you want to be in life.

You are loved beyond your knowledge; you are special just for being you. Whether you believe it or not, I believe you are loved in this world and the next.

My hope for you is:
That you will know that you are loved, always.

That you will be happy and find your own way in life – be fabulous and kind.

Remember you are a spiritual being, whatever that means to you. We all have a soul, emotions, mind, and body; try to look after them all.

You can do whatever you put your mind to; play to your strengths and embrace your weaknesses.

Beware of false friends and be mindful of your choices of partner – whoever he or she may be. You are worthy of unconditional love and must not accept anything less.

There will be times when you slip up and make the wrong decision (you know about mine before I found your Dad). Forgive yourself and start again. There is always another way.

Never give up. When times are hard, look back at the first statement in this list!

Know this, my beautiful girls, I will always tell you the truth. (We've had some funny conversations in the car!) I love you now and always, so does your Dad. You are our lights and joys as well as our stresses! We are your parents, and our role will always be to be there for you and to embarrass you whenever possible! (I now know the fun my parents had while embarrassing me and your auntie!)

I can't wait to see what your futures bring!

All my Love,
Mum
Xxx

Dedication – For my family, in memory of R.M.Wright

7.

Kara Thomas

For My Children

Finley, Ella and Maciee

As I am writing this letter to you today, Finley, you are currently 7 years and 2 months and what an amazing time I have spent with you. Seeing you develop into the amazing little boy that you are today. Ella, you are currently 4 years and 8 months, and it has been wonderful seeing you become this sassy daughter of mine. Maciee, you are currently only 10 months and what a precious 10 months they have been. Bringing you into the world during a global pandemic when Covid19 was discovered in 2020. It's now 2021 and life is crazy as ever.

I want to start off with Finley. Finley, you are my first born my little 8lb 3oz baby boy. I was a young mum when I had you and people said things that weren't so kind but I am so so happy that you were created at that time of my life. Even if it was an early start it means I get to love you longer. You are so amazing, funny, intelligent and handsome, you are my precious little boy and I love you so much more than life itself.

We haven't always had it easy, life has been tough for us from when I had you but I got us through it and I am creating a life for you and your sisters that you all deserve so so much.

Life is going to be hard and you have to go down the right path. I want you to succeed at life and always know that you can talk to me whenever you wish to and whatever it may be about. I am always here for you and will guide you in the best way possible. Listen to others that are trying to help you they may be wise people but always understand that sometimes people aren't so kind and the world is a cruel place. There is crime going on and I really hope you don't get involved with any of that. It isn't a path you will want to go down, it is scary and bad things happen. I have faith in you that you will understand that crime is wrong. Keep yourself to yourself and with friends that are good people and good influents. Don't allow boys or girls to influence you into any bad things. You are better than this and will get further in life if you take the advice mummy has given to you. I only want the best life for you and will try my hardest to make sure you go down the right path and get a good career and achieve your goals in life, whatever they turn out to be. It could be joining the army or becoming a police officer as you keep saying you want to be. You can do this, just set your mind to it and you will go far.

Please have fun and enjoy your less reasonable years. Explore be adventurous and travel, there is so much to the world, more than you could ever imagine. Life is for living and you will need to create your own path sometimes. If that means being alone to grow then understand this is okay, you will grow to the best or what you possibly want yourself to grow into. Mummy will always have your back.

Ella, my tiny 7lb 0.5oz baby girl and Maciee, my big 8lb 9oz baby girl. You girls changed my perspective in life in a way that I knew I had to grow up. Having daughters is amazing but it's hard. I know from being a daughter and a girl myself you will face many challenges. You will be okay if you just ask for advice when you need it and be open and honest about everything. There are things in life that you girls are going to come across and it is going to be scary and emotionally hard to deal with at times. I promise to always be there for you both whenever you need me.

Follow your dreams baby girls you deserve them all. You can achieve anything you want to just believe in yourselves. Ella and Maciee, you are going to come across people that aren't so nice they can be nasty and spiteful. It can be scary sometimes trying to fit into the crowd you aren't born to fit into. That's okay you are your own person and you will fit into what is right for you. Do not make yourself into someone you are not just so you fit in. Create your own crowd it will be much more beautiful.

I want you girls to live the best life you possible can, travel the world, it is amazing. There are so many beautiful countries and nature to explore. Don't settle for anything less than you are both worth. You are both growing into such beautiful, kind and caring daughters of mine. I love you both so much more than you can ever imagine. I will always be here for you, don't ever feel like you can't talk to me. You girls mean the world to me.

Finley, Ella and Maciee, I want you to know that life is not always easy, in fact it is very hard and sometimes you will struggle and feel like you don't understand the way or why. Life is hard and things happen that are out of your control. If I can help you understand some struggles and obstacles that you will face, then hopefully it will make it just that tiniest bit easier for you and answer questions you might have.

You need to always be kind to people, the world will be a better and nicer place if people are nice to one another. This is something that has faded a lot over the years but maybe your generation will bring the kindness that this world needs back. Things are not always how they seem, never judge someone from something you have heard from someone else. You need to make your own observations and treat everyone with respect and you will gain respect back. Always treat your friends and family, even strangers the same way you would want to be treated in return. This is much more pleasant and kind than begin nasty and treating someone in an unpleasant way.

Place yourself around people with positivity and happiness. Don't let other's negative input or negativity contribute to your life and the decisions you make. You need positivity to grow and to have a happy and relaxing life. Make yourself happy first and love yourself because if you are happy and love yourself then that is the main thing. It doesn't matter if somebody isn't happy for you, just be happy for yourself and within yourself. Do not let people hurt you or put you down, you are all perfect to me and amazing in each and every way. Everyone is so different; you all have your own beliefs in life. This is okay because you are your own person and will succeed if you believe you can because you very well can. You can do anything if you just set your mind to it and work hard enough. Don't push yourself too hard, take some time out if need be, that's okay, we all need space sometimes.

The world isn't what it used to be. I mean when I was younger playing out with my friends, coming in when the streetlamp came on was safe but nowadays it isn't so safe. We have much more crime and scary things happening within the world. It's a shame but this is life. Maybe you three will be able to bring this world back to a nicer place. Nowadays we have to wear masks nearly everywhere we go. We aren't allowed to see family or friends and the shops are shut. We have been in lockdown for months; people have lost their jobs and unfortunately loved ones too. It has been hard, it is hard, but we will get through this no matter what. We came together by doing an NHS clap. It's started bringing communities back although that didn't last.

The world has now changed forever, life will never be the same. Large gatherings will always be a risk and the thought of another virus outbreaking will always be a scare. It's so sad that we have lost time but all we can do now is hope for better days to come and I'm very sure they will.

Maciee, even though you were born into this it couldn't have been any more perfect with you. Mummy got the extra snuggles and time with your brother and sister. We went on so many walks and enjoyed the nature that we have. It has really made us value life so much more.

I hope one day when you see this letter it helps you to understand a little bit more than what you do at the time when you're reading this letter. I love you three so much, you will always be in my heart forever.

All my love mummy xxxxx

8.

Kathryn Andrews

To The Four That Make My Heart Flow

To my boy,

My word have we been through some shit! From day one, the day you decided to enter this world it was a struggle. I'd been in labour for a good 8 hours and pushing for some time, when a swarm of nurses and doctors descended upon me, with my legs in the air and all I had to offer on show. I will still never know, even now, 3 kids down, how on earth they expect you to make informed decisions about your labour when you are off your tits and high as a kite, but they do. I was thrust a piece of paper, which I had to sign, to say I agreed to have an emergency caesarean, if that was what it took.

I remember being wheeled down to theatre and once in there, all the doctors and nurses scurrying around, talking over each other trying to tell me what was happening. Then I noticed the forceps, if you don't know what they are, they are like a ginormous kitchen utensil or maybe one you would use at a BBQ, you know the ones I call my pincers that I use to get jars out of the top of the cupboard on the shelves that I cannot reach. Like them. Apparently, they place them either side of the baby's head while mum, me on this occasion, pushes. They tried but still no budging from you. Next, they tried the Ventose. This is basically a Henry hoover with a toilet plunger on the end but looks a bit more clinical, they attach the toilet plunger bit to baby's head and hope that with a light suction and mum's pushing, they can suck the baby out. This didn't work for us either son.

I know at one point they gave me some medicine for something, and my mouth was dry from all the Gas and Air I had been having, and I told the nurse, I can't swallow that because I will be sick, she didn't listen, I took the medicine and then showered her with it with some epic projectile vomiting that you'd usually see in movies. Anyway, by this time we were both more than a little distressed and they decided an emergency caesarean section was the best bet. I basically didn't have any clue you'd been born until I woke up from anaesthetic. Then I was in shock, is this my baby? How do I know this is my baby? Jeez he has got a bit of a cone head. Someone could have swapped him, what if this isn't my baby? He is so bloody cute. My belly has shrunk a bit. Checks nametag, this is my baby. Look how tiny he is. Why does he have sunglasses on? Shit, it hurts when I move, double shit my baby's crying and I can't move!

You were the cutest little boy, with a button nose and the cutest, tiniest fingers and toes, who had been born with jaundice. This still makes me laugh now because Jaundice makes the skin turn yellow and the song that was at number 1 was called colour-blind by a dude called Darius, so the line "feelin yellow" seemed quite appropriate and made me laugh every time I heard it. You had to be in an incubator for a few days, which also meant minimal contact for myself and visitors. When I didn't have any visitors or it was the middle of the night, I had to buzz for a nurse to come and change you or bring you to my bed to feed because the surgery I had to get you into the world had battered my body.

It didn't take me long to get into the swing of things once we were home though, I had chosen to breastfeed and was so proud of myself, a 17-year-old mama breastfeeding her baby. No matter where you needed feeding, I'd whap out my baps, no fucks given and feed my beautiful baby boy. My god did I get some judgement for that, it didn't help I was a teenage mum and I looked it, so the stares and hushed comments were something I quickly learned to shrug off. I was doing what was best for my child and that was all that mattered to me.

My relationship with your dad started to deteriorate, we were together throughout the birth and he was a really good, attentive dad. He helped a lot around the house and worked hard but our relationship was one built on insecurity, violence, and abuse and this went both ways. I gave as good as I got but because your dad was a couple of years older than me, he held all the cards. Everything had to be in his name, the house, the bills, and the money. I was in some senses a kept woman and this would have been great had we lived in the 1950's but I needed some of my own independence. One day there was a conversation between your dad and I around our relationship, it was a gentle conversation, no screaming and shouting, no anger, I cannot for the life of me remember what was said before only his response that was "so you're telling me if we didn't have Levi, we wouldn't be together" and my response which was "yes". From that day forward our lives turned to shit, chaotic shit, emotional shit, depressive shit, argumentative shit, violent shit, any negative shit you could think of right now, that shit and heaps of it.

Now from this point forward, I know you are fully aware of how this story pan's out because you are 18 now, and we have had many conversations around this relationship but there are a few things I want you to know:

Firstly, none of that shit was ever your fault! I never EVER want you to feel as though you are at fault for how any of our relationship turned out or progressed over the years. We both made mistakes, acted on our emotions and frustrations, and ultimately wanted to hurt each other. Never you. So, this is **Lesson 1**: *Never act on an emotional mind*, give yourself time and space to process a situation before you respond. You say things in the heat of the moment that have the capacity to change your whole life projection. Yes, by all means, say what you think or feel but be mindful because **lesson 2**: *delivery is everything*. You can still get your point across in a kinder way but **Lesson 3**: *You can't teach stupid*. Someone who is refusing to see things from someone else's point of view or accept when they are wrong aint ever gunna listen so **Lesson 4**: *Walk away.*

Secondly, Fuck ups are a given, I've made many, you'll make many and so will other people in your life, which leads me on to **Lesson 5**: *Learn from your* *mistakes*. There is a lesson in everything you do and more importantly in every mistake you make, learn your lesson, think about what you'll do differently next time and how you will overcome it. Have a bit of time to mull it over and think about it but **Lesson 6:** *Don't live there.* **Lesson 7:** *Pick your battles.* Yes, it's nice to know your right about something but is there really any point having a disagreement about too much sugar in your coffee or that the grass is green? Not every battle deserves your time or attention. **Lesson 8:** *Know when you are wrong and apologise,* this is no easy task and it takes a lot to not only know when you are wrong but to give a genuine apology. Suck it up buttercup ain't nobody always right but your mama 😊!

Lastly not everyone is going to act as you do or as you expect. Not everyone has had the upbringing, support, or love that you have but that shouldn't stop you from, **Lesson 9:** *Being a good person* Don't let the actions of others deter you from being the person you are, from exuberating kindness and love. There will be people that take your kindness as a weakness, they will take the piss, they may take advantage and that says more about them than it does about you because **Lesson 10: YOU ARE AMAZING!** Keep doing you, you astound me with your resilience, the ability to overcome and adapt, to step out of your comfort zone and achieve whatever you put your mind to.

I can't wait to see what you achieve next in life once all this Corona shit is over and Boris ungrounds us.

We will initiate you to clubbing properly and just know I will always have your back.

Love always,
Mama Bear. xXx

To my girls,

This last 18 months has been so difficult with Coronavirus. I thank god every day that you are now 11 and 13. I don't think I'd have coped very well had you been toddlers. I am so proud of you both with how you have handled this lockdown and worked so hard from home. You have been nothing short of amazing with your commitment to schoolwork and your dedication to your house coats!

You two girls have been my life and soul, with only 18 months between you at times you have been more like worst enemies than sisters but that's to be expected with such a small age difference. It was difficult when the first of you had been born but when the second came along 18 months later, I literally thought my head was about to explode. Juggling all your needs and wants with them of your 7-year-old brothers was a challenge at times. Daddy spent most days working hard to provide for us and spent the evenings and weekends helping me care for all of you. I loved your little quirks and watching you grow and develop your own individual personalities, which brought with them some funny times, although they were not funny at the time. I remember going to the toilet one time and I came downstairs to you both covered in sudocrem – nappy cream. Thick, white cream smothered all over your hands and faces, with mitt prints all over the tv. Then there was the time the older of you two decided to cut the youngers hair, her tight ringlet curls in a heap on the floor, or the time one of you found out where the Christmas presents were hidden and brought them upstairs. I woke up to ripped wrapping paper all over the landing.

You two are such a dynamic duo. Despite your fall outs you always support each other. You love and forgive each other. Even when one of you steals the other's clothes. In no time, you are back friends and thinking about the next prank to play on me and your dad, like covering the toilet with cling film or pretending you have smashed my phone.

As a family we have been through some difficult times, like when Nana passed away. You had to deal without me being around for a little while, but daddy took good care of you. You also had to deal with me when I came home, grieving for my mama. I know that was hard on you, but I want you to know, that on days when I was upset and didn't know how to cope. You pulled me through, both of you, with your fun and games and laughter. That day we sat on the kitchen floor together in streams of tears because Nana was gone forever, you both wrapped your arms around me and gave me the biggest hug, you gave me the strength to carry on and get through the tough days until the tough days were a little less and the fun days were a lot more.

Then Gran died and that brought us all a lot more changes. Our family changed forever from that day forward, we went from a family of 5 to a family of 8 overnight, we had to move to a new house, and all adapt to living differently. I know this was extremely hard for you both and at times I even struggled wondering if we were making the right decision for our family. Now, now I am so glad that we went through that, I am glad that we got the support to come through it. It meant I got to know you both a little bit better on a deeper level. I got to know about your worries, and we worked out a way to tackle them and come through them together. I got to know about your joys, what made you happy but more than anything I got to see your strengths as individuals and as sisters.

You see, that's the thing with having a sister of a similar age, you get to grow up together and enjoy every aspect of life with each other. In difficult times, you get to share those experiences, use each other as sound boards and get advice from one another. In happy times you get to share the laughter and the memories and in mischievous times, you get to prank your family.

You will never have a friend who knows you better than your sister, who drives you just as mad but still loves you unconditionally. A person who has been through all your childhood with you, who loves your crazy and is your personal cheerleader. The one who comes to your aid whenever you are sick or feeling sad. Who will lay beside you on a quilt on the floor to make sure you're not alone throughout the night, who grabs the sick bucket and makes sure you have all you need. If there is one thing I hope for you both, it's that you never forget what a blessing it is to have a sister like yours. To always know the bond you have is unbreakable as long as you both commit to making your sisterhood a priority!

Love you always,
Mama Bear xXx

To my Izmass,

You came into our family as a permanent fixture not too long ago at a time that was difficult for everyone. I know this was not an easy adjustment, but you embraced these adjustments although you found it challenging. I honestly believe that lockdown one helped us all adjust massively to the new family dynamic and I am happy that you continue to embrace this new crazy.

In gaining a new family in us, you also gained being a role model, a role you had never had to navigate before. You have opened your heart and your room to your younger cousins, and I love seeing your relationships blossom with each of them as individuals and as an immensely powerful trio. You really are an amazing role model to them both and I can't thank you enough for taking them both under your wing as you have.

I am constantly amazed by your resilience and although things scare you, you embrace them to better yourself and your understanding of the life you once had, to make a better future for yourself. That niggly self-doubt, I see it creep in but please understand you have the ability, I see it in you. I see it in your persistence when you're going out looking for opportunities that support your future. I see it in your schoolwork and the depth in which you research and compose homework tasks. I see it in your ability to take constructive criticism when you are a clumsy bugger around the kitchen and you're making an explosion competing in the family bake off or the gingerbread house making competition at Christmas.

I applaud your openness with us all as a family and I particularly love and champion the conversations we have in my room when we are all chilling together. Those raw conversations, when we all touch on subjects that are important to us and openly discuss them, they are gold to me. Your vulnerability and honesty in those moments is respected and appreciated. I feel honoured to be a part of those moments and those conversations because your voice matters. Those moments help me feel closer to you and give me a better understanding of you as a person. Your level of maturity is far beyond your years at times and my only hope is that you still find the time to be a teenage girl despite all the pressures that surround you.

I want you to know that you will always have me, and this will always be your home. You are capable of amazing things and I can't wait to watch you flourish and see how your future unfolds. You are so loved; you are beautiful, and you are amazing.

Love you always,

Auntie Kat. xxx

9.

Helen Ingham

Team Ingham... Assemble

To my Babies;

My first born, my daughter, Harriet Esme- the one who made me a mother.

And my second born, my son, Teddy Arthur- the one who taught me strength.

"You're off to great places,
today is your day,
your mountain is waiting,
so get on your way..."
  • *Dr Seuss*

Your Dad and I once agreed when you were little, *"It's not that we don't like who we are now, it's just that we really liked who we were before, too..."* We met in our early twenties, banged teeth when we kissed on our first date, then enjoyed a decade of each other's company before you came along to join us. Your Dad and I are best friends, a great team, a winning match... and You are our legacy of love. You were both born into a happy home full of love and light, a safe place where you will always be welcome and always be encouraged to be and accepted for who you are. We worked hard to build this sanctuary for you, the place that will forever be called 'home'.

Harriet, "Always keep that place inside of you where the magic grows, alive. Don't ever let anyone dull your sparkle."

I write this letter just days before your fifth birthday. You are a vivacious, feisty, loud and fun-loving little girl with the ability to light up a room with your smile. Your laughter is infectious and the most gorgeous sound as you wrinkle your nose to deliver it. We always tell you that your cuddles are the best in the world - you hug with all of your soul and seriously give each embrace your entire everything into it. It's a genuine and affectionate action every single time and I can literally feel all the love inside of you being transferred into me. When you hug someone, you mean it. There is a special, vibrant, love inside of you that you want to share without limits, spreading your inner joy to whomever is lucky enough to be the recipient; heart-warming, comforting and soothing all at the same time.

You have the energy of a lightning bolt, it's as though you appreciate the good in every day and cannot wait to see what each day holds for you. Dad and I often joke about your 'fear of missing out' and the way in which you evade sleep because you think something wonderful might happen in reality whilst you're dreaming. If I could bottle your energy for my own slow days, then I would never need to worry about not getting things done, but you must also remember that your body and mind needs rest between energy in order to keep going at a healthy pace. Rest is good yet something that does not seem to come naturally to you despite my efforts of trying to teach you the importance of slowing down and taking the time to allow yourself to stop. Ignore those who tell you to "just keep going", as that isn't healthy. Stopping/quitting is not the same as failing or giving up. Resting is self-care and showing yourself the kindness that your body deserves. You only get one body for your journey here, and you need to respect it. Whilst you tend to do everything at 100mph, you have earned the nickname 'Queen Faff-a-lot' for your reluctance to do anything you don't really want to do when you're asked to it in favour of some well-timed (on your part) procrastination, a trait you have inherited from both of your parents!

Noise is something you are good at: from the moment you learned to speak you have never stopped. You are at your happiest when you are performing - I wonder if a life in front of an audience awaits you one day? Along with your ability to talk non-stop is your ability to negotiate and argue - such a bright little girl. A persistent child, you tend not to stop until you get what you want. It's one of your best qualities but one of the qualities that drives me the most mad. One day it will take you far but remember to learn the art of losing gracefully and accepting defeat not as a bad thing but as an opportunity to try things from a different angle.

Having recently started school your education is just beginning, and you are thriving. An extrovert amongst your peers, reading and writing seems to be your passion and you have a strong connection to your little group of friends. You have a tendency to mimic the likes and enjoyments of those close to you rather than having the confidence to be yourself, but you're still learning to find your voice of reason and decide upon the things that *you* like without fear of judgement. It will come and when it does, I hope you have the courage to be unashamedly yourself and put two fingers up to anyone who challenges you about it. Your uniqueness is what makes you My Harriet.

Ted, "You are braver than you believe, stronger than you seem and smarter than you think."
At just two-and-a-half years old you have been through more than you will remember, and for your innocence I am thankful. You are a loving, sensitive, playful little man who loves nothing more than sitting in your underwear with a bowl of crisps, watching a screen, at home with your family around you. A proper home-bod it is without doubt the place where you are happiest. Like my little shadow, you tend to follow me wherever I go - I can't leave the room without you attached to me to the point that you have been known to even insist you sit upon my knee whilst I have a poo. We often joke that you'll still be living with us when you're fifty, sitting in your duds eating crisps and watching telly, perfectly content. You too are a social child despite your shyness around new people and you love being with your friends playing.

Your cuddles are warm and tender: you like to stroke my face and pat my back gently just as I do to you when you settle down upon me.

After a rocky start to your sleep pattern (neither you nor your sister let Dad and me sleep for the best part of four years) you relish in weekend lie-ins and breakfast in bed. With a minimum of three dummies (one for each hand and one firmly in your mouth) you like to snuggle and chill, all the while reserving your energy for when the mood hits you to play- then you ramp it up, lively, loud and funny.

At around four weeks old you became poorly with severe reflux. It would torment me, watching you in pain and hearing you cough. Your cry is still one of my worst triggers guaranteed to send my anxiety into a spin. I hope you have absolutely no memory of the pain you were in or the exhaustion you felt, believe me when I say we were mortified at how much of a battering your tiny body took from the acid. But true to your roots, you proved yourself strong and battled through it eventually making it out to the other side. What a relief for us all.

You are my sensitive little boy. Any time you hear or see another child crying your concern for them takes over. If somebody hurts themselves, you will tell me repeatedly about it with the need to try and help in some way. Perhaps a future in healing awaits you? But you must remember my love, that you cannot fix everything. Sometimes you have to be brave and accept that it's okay to walk away from something that causes you distress in order to protect yourself from pain.

My world as your mother is a busy one, yet one that I wouldn't change. Juggling life with children is hard. You arrived with no instructions, yet I was expected to fall into a rhythm and routine that met your needs... it took me a while to figure out that all that really meant was 'love'. Love is all you need, and unconditional love you get without measure every single day. One of my biggest fears and the root of most of my Mum guilt is my anxiety over you potentially ever doubting just how loved you are. Quite often I hear myself reassure you that I can be cross or disappointed with your actions but still love you entirely. Motherly love is an unexplainable feeling, it is nestled deep within my body; I feel it in the pit of my abdomen, where I grew you both from nothing over nine months. I feel it in my heart, which you lie against and listen to. I feel it upon my skin when you touch me, your skin is made from the very same cells. I feel it in my mind, when I sense you aren't happy. It's a beautiful all-consuming feeling of overwhelming pride and protection. My babies, my cubs, my baby birds. Sometimes I worry that I smother you too much with kisses and cuddles, too much for you to feel comfortable with (you two have shown me how suffocating lack of personal space can feel), but I can't help it. I need to feel that I'm showing you how much I adore you in case you can't infer it from my mood or words.

When you were both very little I was poorly. Hormones, sleep deprivation and a personal trauma led my mind to fall apart a bit, yet I struggled through with you two as my purpose, the centre of my world. I want to say I'm sorry for that time. The raised voices, the shouting, the crying, the absence of my words - they were all reactions to how my brain was coping and nothing at all to do with you.

Harriet, I'm so sorry that I changed from being the easy-going Mummy you lived with and got used to for two years into one you didn't recognise, and that you had to adapt to that less capable version of me all over again. I hope I didn't disappoint you.

Ted, I am so sorry that you were denied the capable and happy Mummy that you needed and deserved in your early months. Know that it is one of my deepest regrets. I hope you still felt safe and loved.

I failed, but it was out of my control. I hope I haven't fucked either of you up in the long-term.

Yet through those dark moments you taught me strength. You showed me the importance of self-acceptance and with that the ability to heal and move forwards.

The world is an uncertain place right now, there is a lot going on that you won't yet understand. During my thirty-six years so far much has evolved – technology (please be wary of social media- it isn't real and there is no such thing as perfect despite what people may try to show you), laws, environmentally, educationally. That said, you are being raised as mindful and liberal individuals in a diverse community where we do not judge others and respect our differences - remember to be open minded and to always be kind and considerate. Our planet is going to need help from your generation, please do your part in looking after it however small a contribution that may seem.

With so much confusion I don't want you worry though, you're safe as long as you stick together. Dad and I are your biggest cheerleaders, and you should support each other too. It's never a competition between either of you - you are equals. One day you will stop fighting over who gets to sit on my knee. In each other you have to your advantage the benefit of a ready-made best friend for life should you accept it, possibly the closest and best friend you will ever have. The short age gap between you nearly killed me and your Dad at first, show us that it wasn't the worst idea we've ever had!

I wish for you, success, whatever your own perception of that may be, as long as it makes you happy. No dream is too big if you have the thirst for it - do whatever sets your soul on fire, I want you to be completely happy with the thing you spend most of your time doing (mine is writing).

If you choose a partner, make sure they adore you. Afford them that love and respect in return. I like to think that your Dad and I have set a good example of what being in love means.

Should you choose to one day have your own children then know that they will be your biggest stress but your biggest blessing - I will be here to support you and put my Grandchildren on a pedestal. And if kids aren't for you, then that's fine too. Stay true to your desires and what you want from your life. Be yourself, unashamedly. Work hard but rest in between. There is more to life than achieving the highest grades and being top of the class - all I ask is that you do your best in all your endeavours.

Happiness lies within.

"Life is amazing, then awful, then amazing once again. In between amazing and awful it is ordinary, mundane, routine. Breathe in the amazing. Hold on through the awful. Relax and exhale through the ordinary. That's just living, heart-breaking, soul-healing, amazing, awful, ordinary, life. And it's breathtakingly beautiful." – L.R. Knost

I love you to the moon and back, deeper than the oceans and beyond wherever the butterflies disappear to.

Now go and listen to the song 'Sunscreen' by Baz Lurhman - he will fill you in with the rest of the important stuff.

All my love,
Mum. Xxx

10.

Su Pearson

To My World, My Four Children

Hey there, I just wanted to take the time and sit and write this letter to you all.

Life hasn't been easy for any of you, and I want you to know how truly sorry I am.

I always wanted children, a family and I had visions of how our lives would be, but it never turned out that way.

You see I wanted to give you all a better, happier life then I had growing up, I failed I'm sorry. What I didn't realise or understand was how my childhood had affected me, I didn't understand that I had depression. I just saw myself as a mum who loves her children, feeds, clothes, puts a roof over our heads. You had toys to play with, we went to the park. It wasn't enough, I didn't see it myself or feel it as I felt just like I've always felt, but the depression was bad, although I looked after you, I didn't look after the house, or myself.

2005 social services tore my heart out, they took the best of me away, YOU... I fought so hard to get you home, so hard, but the Judge ruled no. We had contact three times a year for two hours each visit, it was so amazing to see you all but it wasn't long enough, those two hours flew by. Watching you grow even more each visit was hard.

No updated photos sent between visits, no update on how you were, just me sat there crying worrying and missing you all so much.

Those visits where you screamed excitedly "mummy" as you ran towards me for a cuddle filled my heart, I never wanted that cuddle to end.

Here we are today and you're all young adults now and by end of this year you are all free of care orders. You ALL make me so PROUD.

You are all on different journeys in your life, setting up homes, building your careers, I couldn't be any prouder than I am right now.

I hope you can forgive me for letting you down as children, please know I've never stopped loving you.

Keep following your dreams and keep being you.

I hope one day we can sit around the table as a family again.

ALL MY LOVE

Always and forever

Mum xx

11.

Louise T.

My Reasons For Breathing

So, I was wondering how to start this letter and the obvious thing to do was to write a letter as a whole with there being so many of you. I mean I love you all the same, right? But I started thinking that with each of you, there are a bunch different feelings and emotions as well as different experiences that I felt it only fair to address you individually. We are in a pandemic right now and emotions are running higher than usual, so I wanted to put pen to paper and have something for you to look back on, even though you know how much you all mean to me. Just know it has been a privilege to be your mama as I didn't have the best start in life but all I ever wanted was to be a mum... Just promise me one thing, that no matter where life takes you, you will always be there for each other, this is my only wish.

You see…

Jamie

My biggest, beautiful boy. How amazing you are! You, my boy made me a mama 31 years ago at the tender age of 16 when I was just a baby really. I needed you more than I realised, although we are more like brother and sister, lol, well we have fought like it. You were the best thing that had happened in my utterly sad existence. Nobody could take you away from me, you were mine and that made me the most powerful woman on the planet, the fact I had to look after this precious bundle. I was so over-protective and still am even though you are a huge, strong man that does not need mama bears protection.

You were my first true love, and it is those feelings of pure love that led me to have an army of little warriors.

I'm not going to lie, it was hard work and being 16 moving out and being in a marriage at such a young age was so hugely hard, but I fought, I fought for you, to be the best mum I could be. I tried my hardest with the tools I was given, and I know I made some mistakes. Tons of them. But I never gave up and I never, ever stopped loving you.

We have been through lots of tough times and extremely heart-breaking times, but I am so proud of the beautiful human being you are. You are extremely clever and achieve everything you set your mind too. Your job can allow you to work anywhere in the world and I know you would like to go to Canada, so go. Spread those gorgeous wings and fly my boy. When your time is right then have a family, it is never too late. I am so proud of the man you have become too; you respect everyone around you, especially women and I know that your siblings have an absolute diamond to look up to.

Your grandad will be beaming with pride.

Don't let all those negative people influence your decisions. Let them go. They have no place or purpose in your life.

I just hope I've been enough, and I know it was never easy, but I tried to give you all I could, and I could not have loved you any more if I'd have tried.

I love you more with every beat of my heart. Always.

Reach for the stars kid as you were always destined to shine x

Adam

My Taddy, this is probably one of the hardest letters. You're 30 now but I feel like I lost you at 17. You were my side kick, my right-hand man. We were besties and told each other everything. Such a beautiful, sensitive soul. And I still say you should have been in a boy band with that face, lol. As soon as girls came on the scene that was it, lol. Bye mum, lol x You only left home because you had the opportunity of your own place with your brother, and girls and parties turned your head. It would be great. But it wasn't. You went into a relationship and became a dad at a young age and that was toxic so you ran. Where did my Adam go? You weren't you anymore and that broke my heart. We don't see each other often and I'm ok with that now because you like your space, but for such a long, heart-wrenching time I felt broken because you wanted to do you.

You had all those dreams Adam, I want to see you get that spark back and go for it.

Your job at present is a nightmare due to Covid. You're a chef and can't work but it isn't what you want to do. Life is so short angel, please make the most of it.

There is an abundance of help out there for whatever you may need.

I know you don't like us all having opinions about your life but it is only because we care. We only have opinions based on your actions because your actions affect us all.

I want to see you soar, I want to see you happy and I want to see you be the best man you can be because you are so beautiful. You can still be a great dad. It's never too late.

I love you so much Adam, that will never change.

I'll be here for you always x

Jordan

This story right here has to rip my heart right out. My absolute joy, what a lucky mum I am you know. I have always known I am blessed with you all but just knowing I have you here is all my dreams come true.

The story of almost losing you at 3 years old is only known within our circle. You see when you drowned, and you had to be brought back to life right in front of me, it will forever haunt me. I still have night terrors 23 years on, and I have to thank God daily for allowing me to keep you. I will never ever get over that day. Being in a foreign country with no support. Living in hospital all week with you in a high dependency ward while my other boys were trying to enjoy the rest of their holiday. Your big brother saved you, along with the fireman on holiday. Such a lucky mum and such a lucky boy.

You are one of my best friends and I am so grateful to be so close to you. Probably coz you have no choice as I don't want to lose you again, lol.

You are such a handsome, loving, beautiful boy and the best big bro to the younger ones. I love the bond you have with the youngest and the way your sister terrorises you is the funniest thing and yet I am so grateful to witness this.

I am actually finding it hard to write this as it is so overwhelming how I am feeling, thinking about you.

You are amazing. You are absolutely smashing your career and what you set out to achieve is just unbelievable as you are getting better and better. So proud of you and just keep being you. Such a beautiful, caring and generous human. I am so proud of the way I have raised my men.

You know I love you and know how much x Again, I hope I've been enough x

Love you forever my beaut
Always x

Brandon

Aww my little special care dude. Born 7 weeks early but bounced right back. Such a gorgeous, funny, generous boy you are my Brandon-Lee. At 24 you don't take life too seriously and I love that. You were such a funny little man, and I can see you in your little boy. I know the last 2 years have been a nightmare, but you are amazing. You have just dealt with it and been the best dad you can be.

You see, I know you never wanted kids. Think I kinda put you off haha. But life has a funny way of smacking you in the face. You've had your fair share of heartbreak, but you have coped. I think you are just the best dad and just know it won't always be hard. He adores you and that is just testament of how much love you show him. Plus, he is ridiculously spoilt.

We always know when you're at home, coz if Reuben isn't screaming his head off then we can hear you, lol. I wouldn't change that coz I love your energy. The things you come out with have me in stitches.

You always spoil your mama and always think outside the box. Thank you for being you. You are such a loving, generous and beautiful man. Thank you for being respectful to me and thank you for respecting others x

Another true diamond I have created, and anybody should be thanking their lucky stars to have you in their lives.

Love you always and forever gorgeous boy x

CJ

"Love you mum" will forever ring in my ears, lol. Usually, a daily occurrence when you're being annoying or winding me up, lol. My little Rick Astley. You have just turned 18 and the eldest of me and your dad's. I kind of want to apologise that you haven't got much of a family outside our bubble but think we do ok. Sorry you don't get 2 birthdays or 2 Christmas's like the older boys lol. I know you want them ha x but it aint happening kid. You are such a sweet boy, and I know you think my fave, lol. I love you, you know that, but you need to move more and get off your bed, haha.

Seriously though you are doing so amazing, and I know because of the lockdowns it has been hard to smash your course in college. You have done what you can and am so proud of you, coz it is really hard, especially when you can't really learn engineering through a laptop. Now you're on the road to University to study Aeronautical engineering and oh my! My first to go to Uni and I could burst with pride. However, this comes at a cost. You may be flying the nest and I can't deal with not seeing your head every day.

I want you to know that, if I'm not around one day, then just remember how much you were loved and wanted. I am truly sorry that you got your dad's name, but he was excited at getting his first boy. Please forgive me, lol.

I truly love you CJ and I hope for nothing but the best for you. Don't stop believing in yourself because I never will. Oh, and forever be a mummy's boy lol.

You are a superstar, and superstars' soar.

Love you kid x Always x

Corey

Corey Luke, my beautiful blue-eyed boy. How I wish you could see yourself as I do. You were the most amazing baby. Named after my love of "Lost Boys". Rarely cried. Just smiled and laughed all day every day and grew up to be such a comedian. So, so handsome with your curly blonde hair. All was good until you started high school and following the wrong crowd got you into all sorts of mischief.

Being an extremely loyal friend did you no favours as you took the fall a lot. As you progressed through the years, the stress and heartache caused was immense, trying to ensure you followed a different path than the ones your gang of friends did. I know how hard it's been, and I feel for you I really do, but by following a different path has allowed you to keep out of trouble.

You faced so many challenges in school and hated it, but you went in, every day and stuck to it and I couldn't be prouder of you.

You're almost 17 and in college training to be an electrician. Again, it's been hard with lockdown, but you've absolutely smashed it.

I have seen such a change in you over this last year and you are even more beautiful than you were. You have so many dreams and you want to be successful. I bet my life you will be. You have taken Brodie under your wing and I love seeing that. As much as you wind him up, he really looks up to you.

Going forward I want you to reach for those dreams and be the greatest 'spark' ever. Everyone needs an electrician in their lives, lol x Keep going gorgeous boy, I am super proud of you my beautiful Corey Luke.

I love you beyond measure x
Always x

Kenzie

My chunky monkey, my lucky number 7. You were such a happy smiley kid who loved singing Abba with mama, lol. Think you were as tall as me by the time you were 6, haha. Proper mummies boy till high school. 15 going on 30 you are, coz you love making a cocktail so I'm thinking you're probably going to have a bar job on the side. Such a good boy, well just not in school coz the teachers don't like a joker. Another diamond in the making. Don't ever change being you though because you are so beautiful, inside and out.

Having you three boys so close in age was like having triplets but one of the best stages in my life, even though you have brought so much boyish trouble. Broken arms, eye trauma from a nerf gun and climbing up a tree and your brother falling off. My word did A&E have their work cut out.

You used to love cooking and I know you're awesome at it. Please don't stop just coz I'm your maid and chef, lol.

You were supposed to be taking your exams but again can't. It is what it is but whatever you do after school and in college I am sure you will excel at. I know at the moment you've applied for Army college and I can't tell you how scared and proud I am at the same time. What am I going to do without you? you give us the laughs and the banter. You're not even 16 yet and wanting to go away, my heart won't cope, but I want you to be the best you can be and of that I am sure of.

You were made to be awesome young man and don't ever forget that.

You make me smile every day, so, so proud of you.

I love you sonshine x
Forever x

Tiana Seren

Well, my Queen, my first girl after 7 sons. My sensitive, shy, funny, quirky, mini me. You've heard the story so many times about how wanted you were and how you came to be yet it still seems surreal. Yet here you are, 13, hormonal and K pop's biggest fan. I remember lavishing you in so much pink stuff it was even too overwhelming for me, lol. You grew up to hate pink and anything girly, haha, my bad! Such a tomboy yet you have the most amazing, red, long hair that is your pride and joy. You're the giggler of the family and if you don't chuckle at yourself daily then there's something wrong.

I think I thought that the dynamics would change a lot in the house after having you, they did slightly but for the better. You make me smile every day and you're just a beautiful soul. Make sure you look after your little sis; you will forever need each other.

You're so shy but once you come out of your shell, you are so funny. I know you're experiencing some challenges at the minute but me and your dad will be here for you as long as we can be.

My girl, I want you to have the world and always know that mama has your back. Never, ever let anybody take anything from you. I want you to become a strong, fierce, independent woman and with all your big brothers behind you god help your boyfriends, lol.

I adore you, my beautiful girl. Live your best life and thank you for choosing me to be your mama x Angel of mine X

I love you Queen x
Always x

Saffia Jasmine Rose

When I first got pregnant, I just knew I was having another princess. My beautiful, gorgeous girl, you made a dramatic entrance into this world and almost 10 years on you still rule. What an absolute joy you have been. You have been the sassiest, funniest and cheekiest kid ever. With your love of makeup, nails and everything pink and fluffy, you are definitely the yin to Tiana's yang. I love the bond you girls have, as much as Ti can be annoying please stay the best of friends, girls need to stick together.

You absolutely make my day every day. Your dad absolutely loves his boys but my goodness, nothing comes close to his girls. You girls are so lucky to have 8 brothers to look out for you and love you. You have the boys wrapped around your little finger, always have had and it is absolutely hysterical to watch. I feel so sorry for any boy that comes into your life.

You love your snapchat filters and your Tik Tok videos and I just know you will make it in this world. This lockdown has knocked your confidence but get up my girl and stand proud.

You are my sunshine on a rainy day, and I never tire of seeing your stunning smile. I can't wait to see you grow into a beautiful woman, but for now I am just enjoying seeing you grow.

Reach for those stars' angel, they are yours for the taking.

Love you forever princess x My Girl x
Always x

Brodie Cole

Last but not least my baby boy, my lil bear cub. How I love you. I always had a dream that I had a 10th baby, and you were a boy. So, when I got pregnant, I just knew. The first 3 years were quite tough as we had to fight the hospital for something that happened to you. But my boy we won. You were so clingy to me and it's only this last year that you have your own room and have decided you like it and are not joined at my hip, haha. You're 7 now and I have noticed how you have changed, the moody side is coming out now, yayyy!!

This home-schooling lark is taking its toll and I know you have struggled, but I know your capabilities and I don't push you. You are such a bright boy, and I am sure you will find yourself once again when you get back to school.

I want to see you smile again when I pick you up from school or when I come in through the door. You see me 24/7 and I know you don't want to go back. This time round, lockdown has been harder, but I am cherishing this time that I have with you. Had with you all.

There is so much love for you little man that I am positive you will do great things with all these amazing mentors to look up to. Stay cuddly.

I hope you grow up knowing how much I love you, you're my baby Bear and I love you more, most, more than most and more than everything x

Always x

All My Love
Mama x

12.

Zara Jones

Hard Times, But Easy To Love

My Darlings,

I wanted to pause in the craziness and take a moment to write you a letter, yes, a letter may seem old fashioned to you now BUT it is something you can (hopefully) treasure forever.

I was going to write individual letters, but the same thing would be said, so I thought I would write one that you could read together. Here it goes.

Could I first start by apologising that you've had to spend two birthdays in lockdown? Mammy wasn't being mean and making up some silly thing to avoid a party for you, the virus was real (look it up) however much I hated all the cooking, prep, sorting the party bags, stressing and panic for a party (especially the one-time daddy put the wrong time on the invitations and mammy had to tell everyone to come back in an hour). I loved seeing your faces light up, the joy and excitement on your faces made it all worthwhile. But we are genuinely not allowed to meet up in mass and certainly no parties (so I'll forgive all the times you may have thrown that in my face growing up lol if you haven't............you're awesome thank you).

I've not been the best Mam to you, I know that, and I apologise. If I could work Daddy would be home more rather than out working all the time (I'm so so sorry for that, this isn't the life I chose for myself). I hate seeing you upset because Daddy won't be home in time to tuck you into bed and kiss you goodnight, but I will always send him up to do just that when he's home. Daddy loves you very, very much and misses you too and is always sad when he's not able to be here in time. (Again, I apologise to you all, I wish I could change it, hopefully one day I'll be cured, and we'll swap lol).

Growing up watching all of your friends have beautiful things and fancy holidays can't have been easy. But I want you to know, I did my best, I tried so very hard. All those camping trips may not have been much, but I put my absolute all into them. I tried to teach you the skills I learnt growing up, not just from cadets but from my mam and dad, nan and daddo. Skills I thought would benefit you in situations life throws at you when you don't expect it. I clenched my teeth to fight the pain and smiled so you wouldn't know the pain and upset I was in. Those trips to the beach, sandy toes, ice cream covered faces, plastic buckets and spades, salt-stained t-shirts, countless goes on the teacups, ghost train and other rides, were all so you could have wonderful memories of a Mam and Dad that tried to give you an adventure and fun no matter how close to home.

Daddy and I went through a lot to have you, you are our miracles... Literally. The pain, struggle, worry, fight, blunders, tears and screams were all worth it because they gave us you. Our missing pieces. You completed our puzzle, our hearts, our souls. Not only ours, but also your Mamma and Daddo's. You saved us all, brought us back to life. Filled us with more joy and love than we ever could have imagined. I wouldn't change that for the world, none of us would.

I may have gone through life hating how I look and how little I can do, but my word, I'd do it again in a heartbeat if it meant having you. As I watch you grow, I am filled with so much pride and admiration. I am in awe of you, your confidence, abilities, zest for life and sheer guts to try something. You make us all very proud.

I want you to know, to me love isn't the money you spend, it's the love you give and time you spend. (yes, I know I'm contradicting myself as I wish I could have given you more, but I gave you everything I had and even what I didn't have no matter how big or small) but what you never went without was love. You can always make money; you can't make time. I so hope you understand this and carry it forward with you with your children. You can have the luxuries, working hard but make sure your loved ones know you love them unconditionally, and your time is theirs.

I hope you grow up never knowing how much I hated myself, how much I wished for better and more for you (not just money). I hope you grow up knowing that you are my two eyes, my heart, my soul, my world, my universe. I have always wanted you, ever since I was little. I vividly remember asking Santa for a baby when I was small, he brought me a doll and I was so disappointed. Not in an ungrateful way (I very much loved my doll and took care of it for years) but because it wasn't you. It wasn't a child I could nurture and love, someone that would look at me how I looked at my mother (and father) ... Full of love, admiration, awe and wonder. When you arrived all my Christmases came at once, you completed me in the way I'd been waiting for all those years. It seems so cruel now to have lumped you with me as a mother, but I couldn't not have you, no matter the struggle. I truly hope the stigma of having a poorly mother hasn't affected you deeply. The world can be so cruel and judgmental, I've tried to shield you from it but also teach you, a disability doesn't define the love you can give. Being different isn't anything to be ashamed of or point and stare at. Love is love, it has no colour, gender, ability, disability, agenda or explanation, don't ever forget that.

I often sit and watch you sleeping, hoping that life is kind to you, that you work hard and go through life with grit and determination. Remember what I always said, if at first you don't succeed, try, try, try again. That goes no matter how old you are. Dreams can be a reality if you knuckle down and push for them. I want nothing but the world for you and I'm sorry I'm unable to provide that (but I can give you my unconditional love and my time because my darlings you are worth every second of my time and drop of my love).

At the time I am writing this, we are sat in our second lockdown. Second round of mammy trying her best to home-school you and keep you entertained (while keeping myself sane). I know I've pushed you, bribed you to finish one more piece for the day, at times shouted (sorry for that) and others not bothered with work for the day (also sorry for that) but I did it all for you. So that you wouldn't fall behind (believe me it's not been easy translating back and fore from Welsh to English, English to Welsh with brain fog lol).

The future holds so much for you. I wish nothing but the absolute best for you, always have, always will. I can't begin to put into words how much I love you, how much you complete me, how you saved me. I've so enjoy watching you grow, develop personalities, learn, stumble and fall and get back up again and mature. I'm not perfect, but then again who is? But no matter what, I will always be your champion, cheerleader, shoulder to cry on, ear to complain to, arms to embrace you, warmth when you need it, guidance when you seek it, advice (even when you don't think you need it), confidante, first aider, best friend, well-wisher, good luck chanter, defender, monster fighter (even when you're too old to think there's a monster under your bed), tie straightener, hair tidier, teacher (even if there's no more lockdowns) have a tissue ready to wipe your tears away and above all, I will ALWAYS be your mam, nothing will ever change that not on earth or even in the stars.

Life's not always going to be fair, or go your way, or the way you would like it to. But that doesn't mean you roll over and give up. I've tried to shield you from as much as possible but some things I can't shield you from. Be as ready as you can for those. Be kind. Make good choices and you'll be ok.

As you go forward with life please remember, NEVER go to sleep on an argument, ALWAYS remember to kiss and make up. You ARE worthy, you ARE loved, and you ARE amazing. I never fully understood or believed those words that were said to me many times growing up until I had you, suddenly they made sense, they were real. I didn't realise how deeply and unconditionally someone could love until I had you. Don't get me wrong I love your daddy, but my love for you is so different. It's deeper, it's more powerful, fearless, effortless and pure. You will know this one day, don't be scared of it (even though it can be scary) embrace it and enjoy it because who knows how long we'll have it for.

Fight hard my Darlings, love unforgivingly and unconditionally, be silly, be happy, be caring, be careful and have fun. Never forget your worth to me. Never question or forget my love for you. Please go forward with what I have instilled in you, never judge a book by its cover, never discriminate, no one is better than you, your best is all we can ask for, don't judge what you don't understand, don't be afraid to ask questions, be bold, be brave, be kind, be you. No matter who you love, whatever your destiny is, wherever life takes you, wherever love takes you, know that Daddy, Mamma, Daddo and I are so very, very, very proud of you. Never forget that. Look in the mirror and know the face staring back at you is one that is loved more than you will ever know and is truly beautiful and kind inside and out. You are my pride and joy, my greatest achievement, the apples of my eyes, YOU are my legacy.

I love you to the moon and stars and back, to infinity and beyond, forever and ever. Amen. Beat you lol.

ALL MY LOVE
ALWAYS
Mammy
XXXXXXXXXXXXXXXXXXXXXXXXX

13.

Chelsea Canoncico

Dear Girls,

I know I haven't been there since the beginning, but it doesn't change how much I love you. I know that our lives have been very non-traditional and that's what makes our bond so much stronger. I will always love you. I feel like you ladies have a good handle on what love is so far but just in case. Please, please, please remember that love is not just someone showing you attention. Bad attention is not love.

Love is not being convinced to do something, anything you're not comfortable with. Love is respecting yourself and knowing your boundaries. Love is the people who always care and will always be there for you, the people who show up for you emotionally, physically and mentally.

Remember we all love differently too, while I can show you I love you by getting you things I know you like, others might show you they love you by making you dinner. Know yourself, what you love to do and think of how you show others.

I'll always be here, your Ma and Pa, all of your aunts and uncles, your siblings...we'll be here for you.

Love,
Mom

To My Son,

Oh my boy, how you've taught me love. You've taught me to love myself, my body and my personality. You've taught me that love is something I can choose to give and receive but that there is no love bond like a mom to her son.

The day I found out I was pregnant; I couldn't believe it. The day I gave birth to you made me realize that I would do anything for you. I felt this overwhelming love like no other. Nothing I've ever felt from someone else, from something else or myself.

As you've grown, I have too, and I know that I will always love you. I will not agree with you all the time but that doesn't mean I do not love you. You helped me and continue to help me grow in ways I never knew I needed.

Love,
Mom

As you all grow you need to remember a few things. Love yourself first, love yourself the most and if for some reason you can't love yourself at the time; find one thing you can love about yourself at that time and love it.

Love is not something you can expect from the world. The world is scary, ugly and changes so fast that it can be completely different in a day. Loving yourself first won't change. If you learn to truly love yourself first, you are less likely to fall for the first person to show you attention or affection.

Loving yourself means knowing your worth and knowing what everyone around you is worth. To treat others with respect is love and to show respect is love. Know your boundaries and respect them. Know your morals and your values, that is loving yourself. Staying within those guidelines for yourself is love.

OH and in case no one told you, those people on magazine covers are airbrushed.

14.

Vicky Robinson

To The Ones Who Fill My Heart With Love

Dear Lewis, my rainbow baby.

On the day of my Hen party, still running around making the final preparations to my forthcoming wedding to your dad, I knew I felt different. Although I'd just miscarried our baby the month before, the doctor had told us that a woman is most fertile after losing a baby. I was desperate for a baby of my own, and it seemed so wrong to try and conceive after a miscarriage, but it also felt so right.

I still had pregnancy tests in the bathroom, so off I went to pee on the stick. Two minutes later a smiley face beamed back at me, confirming to me that I was pregnant. It wasn't enough though; I still didn't believe it. I went to Tesco and bought more tests; I even asked the pharmacist if it was possible to get a false positive result. I couldn't believe my luck, the Hen night, the wedding paled into insignificance now. When I looked at my record in the hospital, my GP had written that I was incredibly happy to be pregnant, and that I had already taken 7 pregnancy tests just to make sure. It didn't stop there; I would continue to take pregnancy tests as I was so scared of losing you.

Of course, the worrying started straight away, what if I had another miscarriage? I couldn't bear the thought. It was my Hen party; how would I get through it without everyone noticing that I wasn't drinking? I had to pretend I was drinking vodka all night as it was clear like the actual water I was really drinking. I wasn't taking any chances.

As you know, I electrocuted myself on the plug of a submersible pump, after the pipe froze and water began to flood the cellar, where the washing machine lived. Everyone told me not to worry but worrying was my forte. I called the hospital and they told me to come in to be monitored, just in case. Your dad and I headed for the hospital; I was in bits. Apparently, we were lucky, everything was fine. I didn't feel very lucky, I left the hospital a bag of nerves. I bought my own heart rate machine and sometimes spent hours trying to find your heartbeat, which sounded like the chug of a train. It sometimes caused me increased fear if I couldn't find your heartbeat, even though I knew that, to the inexperienced, untrained mum to be, with a home heartbeat machine, it was always going to be difficult.

At 36 weeks pregnant I happened to tell the midwife that I had been itching on my hands and feet, mainly at night. The next thing I know I'm rushed in for a blood test which confirmed I had Obstetric Cholestasis. I knew nothing about this random condition, which actually meant that I had liver disease. Not only that, but I also had to take medication and would have to be induced early, as babies can be delivered stillborn if left to term.

I was induced at 39 weeks, the contractions came hard and I felt as though I was being winded, over and over again. I had gas and air, pethidine and an epidural. I slept for 12 hours, and as I woke, I asked what everyone was waiting for. Apparently, they were waiting for me. You had turned your face sideways so I had to lay on my side for half an hour to try and get you to move, then when it came to the time to push, they had given me that many drugs I couldn't feel the contractions. The midwife was not happy with me. I almost had to have a caesarean, but they decided to cut me and pull you out instead. As they dragged you away, the alarms began to sound, and it felt like half of the hospital had entered my room. My dignity went out of the window as the plight for my baby's life was on. At last, you screamed, and it was the best scream I had ever heard. My heart burst with love, as you were placed in a see-through cot next to me. We stared at each other from our beds, I felt like the luckiest woman alive.

Why did I need to tell you that, I hear you cry? From the moment you were conceived, my job as your protector kicked in. I would do anything for you, absolutely anything. I quit smoking, I quit drinking, I ate healthy meals every day, I took my multivitamins, I went to every antenatal class. I did everything I could to ensure my womb was the best home for you, until I could hold you in my arms and give you the best family home. You were wanted, more than anything in the world and I can't tell you that enough.

Your dad already had a daughter, so he wasn't as nervous as I. I panicked about everything. When I couldn't breastfeed you, it was the first of many times when I felt like I had failed you. The first day at nursery, you threw a chair at a teaching assistant because she asked you to tidy up. I felt guilty for sending you to nursery, I thought it meant that you were unhappy or scared. Your dad had a very different approach than me when it came to discipline, he was very strict, and I just wasn't. Your dad and I parted ways, you were nearly 4. A year later we were divorced.

I overcompensated for your missing dad, although he was still around, I felt a massive amount of guilt. I wanted you to have a perfect family, not a broken home. My mum and dad (Grandma and Grandad) were still together, I felt like I had failed you again. It has been a difficult journey for both of us and there are many things I regret as your mum. Being a single parent was tough, I didn't like to be alone which meant I sometimes brought my boyfriends into your life. Even though I thought it was the right time, it often turned sour, and we were back alone again.

There are a few occasions that I will never get over, the memory of the blue jumper and the memory of the bannister still haunt me to this day. I wasn't always a good role model for you, purely because I am human, and I make mistakes. As parents, we try to help children to not make the same mistakes as us, however, I also understand that it is unrealistic to believe that anyone can do that. You will make your own mistakes, but when you do, I will always be here for you, no matter what.

From the age of 3, you always had problems in school. You struggled with your work and your behaviour. The older you became, the further the difficulties became prominent. I battled with your Primary School, as at first, they didn't agree that your behaviour was of any concern. However, in Year 3, I had stopped watching you for 30 seconds in the playground at school. The next thing I hear is kids shouting. I turn around and find that you were fighting with a boy in Year 5. At that moment, my world fell apart. I walked you into school and I cried to the Headteacher. I needed help, I could not watch my little boy fighting, it hurt me to think that you could have been hurt. Things started to happen, you had an Individual Learning Plan with the school, and they had an Educational Psychologist to come and assess you. This was the start of our ever-long battle to get you the support you needed.

My parenting was always under scrutiny, I had done every parenting programme I was told to do, I had been referred to every service going, ultimately, the common theme from each service we went through, was that it was all down to me and my lack of parenting skills. Eventually, the services decided that you had complex needs, having traits of lots of different things, such as Autism and ADHD, as well as hypermobility in your left hand and a slow processing speed. I single-handedly fought the system to get you to be in the right Secondary School, a mainstream school with a specialist provision, who would give you the support that you had required all along. Your answer was always, "I never asked you to do that", and my response was always, "I'm your mum, I will fight for you every single day, that's my job". The guilt never left me, I internalized the fact that everyone thought it was my parenting that had failed you and that broke my heart.

We've had our arguments and fights, but we have always been there for one another. You have always had such a low opinion of yourself and no matter how many times I praise you, it never seems to sink in. I am so proud of you Lewis, Lewsham, Hammy, Lewbert, Leo and all the other nicknames we have given you over the years. I wish you could see how much of a wonderful, kind, loving person you are. When your sister was in hospital and you had to live with Grandma and Grandad for 7 weeks so I could go to Germany for her Proton Beam Therapy, you were incredibly brave. You had to start Secondary School without your mum there. My heart missed you so much, but I was glad that you were able to come out and see us in Germany a few times. The very fact that you suffer with anxiety must have made this time an incredibly difficult time for you.

I love our drives in the car, when you were younger, we would sing songs and radio advert jingles at the top of our voices. Now you're 14 and way to cool to do that, we take it in turns to pick songs and play and sing them really loud. Take That – Rule the World will always be our song, even though it says, "if you stay with me girl, we can rule the world". I changed the words to boy when you were little and sang it to you all of the time. I literally felt that with you, my life was complete, and we could achieve anything.

You are growing into a handsome young man and even though you're not academic, you are incredibly intelligent and skilful, in many areas of life. Although you love to wind people up, mostly your older and younger sisters, you would also do anything for them.

Lewis, I have and will always fight for you, no matter what. I love you to infinity and beyond and love to watch the stars with you, trying to figure out the shapes and wishing upon a shooting star. I love chasing after cars I know you like, just so I can send you the photo. I love how you let me link your arm when we are walking, because I'm more scared of crossing a road than you. I love how honest and open you are with me, even when you know I might give you a bit of a lecture. I love that even though you are young, you have so many important morals and values which will hold you in good stead for the future. Despite your difficulties and how adults have often misjudged both you and I, we have stuck together and shown them that at least we can be honest about being a real family, with real issues, we don't think we are better than anyone else, we don't criticise other people. We are who we are and although being judged hurts, it always says more about the person who is doing the judging than the people who are being judged. So, walk tall, keep your head held high, and remember that you are an amazing person with so much to give. Any person will be lucky to have you in their lives.

I love you, Mum (I know you're too cool for Mummy) xxx

Dear Amelia, my Superhero.

I know how you hate me calling you a Superhero, you would prefer Unicorn Princess, or even Spot, the feral child from the movie 'Good Dinosaur'.

Whenever we call you Spot, you howl, awwooooo just like in the movie. I called you Spot because you are your own person, you don't care what people think, you want to be free, running and jumping in muddy puddles, running around the house naked looking like nobody's child because you hate your hair being brushed. I love that about you.

I call you Superhero because you are the bravest girl I know. You started Nursery not speaking to anyone, you would eventually whisper to a few of your friends, but if an adult looked at you, you would immediately stop. They almost referred you to Speech and Language therapy till I filmed you talking in the car none stop to me. No one believed that you could talk. The selective mutism turned into a stubbornness to just not speak to certain people, usually males, but always strangers. Supermarket cashiers would try to talk to you, whilst I was packing the bags and you would just ignore them. However, I knew it was coming partly from a place of shyness, as I myself was shy too.

At the age of 4, after having a seizure in school, you were diagnosed with a cancerous brain tumour. I won't go into that here as that's another story, one you'll be able to read one day, but needless to say, our world fell apart. That shy, 4-year-old girl grew into a girl that did not fear hospitals, you bravely walked the corridors and wards, as if they were your own. You were only interested in all of the new toys you now had to play with in the hospital, and we spent so much time in the playrooms. You woke up from brain surgery and asked if you could go and play. We stared at you, you had a huge bandage around your head, wires coming from all areas of your body, a bruised face and a catheter, and after 9 long hours in surgery, all you wanted to do was play. The only thing you complained about was the white Calpol, which you completely refused to take. You demanded that they went and found pink Calpol and, after running around for an hour trying to get a prescription, you finally got the pink Calpol.

We had to take you to Germany so you could have Proton Beam Therapy, for 7 whole weeks. The hospital was immaculate, the staff spoke some English but were sometimes hard to understand. After the hospital staff accidentally popped your PIC Line, the tube where sedatives were administered so you could be asleep for the proton procedure, we decided to see if you could manage it awake. The hospital didn't usually allow under 5's to have proton therapy awake, however, the alternative was a chest port, which meant you would have to undergo a big operation to install the port, which would scar you for life.

Every day we watched you take the hands of the hospital staff, as they led you through those double doors that closed tightly behind you. We never understood how you managed it, it was like you developed an unspoken connection. The hospital staff communicated trust and safety in their body language, as you equally put your trust in them. You managed to lay still for 30 minutes, with the help of a moulded mask that pinned your head down, as the Proton Beam worked its magic. Even the word superhero does not fully describe how brave you were, how brave you are, every single day. You never cared that you had a bald patch of hair, where you had brain surgery. You eventually went back to school like you had never been away. The left sided weakness you had, due to the surgery did not even require physiotherapy. You were determined to get up and walk, ride the toy car around the hospital and colour. As you are left-handed, it could have caused some serious problems, however you rose to the challenge and within days you would never have known there was a weakness.

Even now you love to go to the hospital, to have a ride on Lunar Jim, get an ice cream from the vending machine, spend a fortune in the little shop and have us walk to the opposite end of the hospital, so you can run up and down over the bridge. You never liked the cannulas which were needed to inject dye into your body halfway through the MRI scan. Yet you managed to lay in the MRI machine, awake for an hour, watching a film on the upside down tv, that was the right way around for you, as you watched through the mirror. Again, children your age were put to sleep for an MRI, but not you. You weren't going to miss the chance to watch a film or have a nap, as the machine beeped noisily around you.

I truly believe that your stubbornness, as most people called it, is actually your strong will and determination to be who you are, get what you want and to stay positive, even in the dark times. Even though you still, at 7 years old, refuse to talk to certain people, demand that we do things for you, right now, get bored if you're not playing for more than 5 minutes and talk incessantly, at home with us, and with friends, you show your strength. I can imagine you as a manager, delegating tasks, pretending that you are boss like, when underneath there's that caring, loving, empathic nature.

We are two years in to a 5-year wait, for an all clear from the cancer. It has been the hardest, most arduous, terrifying, painful time of our lives. Words can't even describe how hard it has been, yet I'm grateful. I'm grateful that I can think about your future and what it might look like, I'm grateful to be able to hold you, love you and still have you here. Parenting, without a doubt, is one of the hardest jobs in the world, but it seems easier now we have faced the worst. The little things that would have bothered me before, now seem insignificant. People say I spoil my children, but it no longer bothers me because I know how grateful I am to have you and your brother here. Until people face what we have faced, it's impossible to know how you will react.

Amelia, you are my superhero, my inspiration, my pillar of strength, my determined, strong willed little unicorn princess. You have shown me that you can get through anything if you stay focused on the positives. Of course, I've heard of play therapy, but I never fully understood the true therapeutic value of it. I spent hours watching you play in the different hospitals, and without knowing I sat for ages, colouring printed pictures for the children. Now we colour together.

The gold, silicone ring that dangles on my necklace, next to the fingerprint charms of you and your brother, has inscribed the words, 'Amelia my hero'. I love you more.

I love you, Mummy xxx

Dear Elise,

Firstly, I want to tell you how happy I am that you have come back into my life after 10 years. You are a beautiful, 18-year-old woman now and, I couldn't be prouder of you. After your dad and I divorced, there wasn't an option to still see you or have a relationship with you, but I want you to know that I always kept tabs on you. When your dad and I were getting along, I would ask how you were and what you were up to. Your dad once asked me, after we had divorced, to make a phone call, to ensure that services were arranging a joint meeting to support you. I was always good at talking to professionals, due to my job and I was so happy to oblige. I don't know what you believed, but I want you to know that I always wanted to be a part of your life.

We have recently recounted many memories that we have of your childhood, and some that you have forgotten. Of course, your story is your story, and not for me to tell. This letter is to let you know that I have always considered you as my stepchild, even though your dad and I were divorced, even though he re-married and his wife adopted you. You always had a piece of my heart. It wasn't until recently that I told you just how many people were looking out for you, and thinking about you, without you even knowing who some of them were. I talked about you often.

I feel like I have been able to help you put some of the pieces of your childhood together, however small they are. I feel like we have renewed a relationship that is now stronger than ever, and I love how honest and authentic you are. You're not afraid to talk to us about anything and it makes me so happy that you trust me to listen to you, non–judgmentally.

When you tell me things you have remembered about your childhood, it takes all my strength not to break down in front of you. I sometimes feel like it's not my place to break down, it's your story, not mine. I was a part of it, granted, and we did all we could to keep you safe, but I often feel like I failed you. It just hurts me so much, especially when you said you felt like you had lost lots of mums, I wanted to cry. I never wanted you to feel like you had lost me. You have so many people in your life that love you.

You have so many good qualities and I don't think you see them as much as you should. You are a bright, beautiful, chatty, down to earth person, who puts everyone at ease in your presence. You are genuine, authentic and kind, you're so wise beyond your years. You are strong, yet not afraid to show your vulnerabilities. I am amazed at your confidence; I wish I had been as confident as you at your age.

I know there are a lot of expectations placed on you from others, and that these can become overwhelming sometimes. You are still young, and you will make mistakes along the way, we all do. I believe that things happen when we need them to happen the most, and you Elise, will have your special day. You will figure out what you want to do and who you want to be, in time. Don't pressure yourself into conforming to the wishes of others. Stay true to yourself and you will be happy. We all want what's best for you, but only you get to decide what that is.

You've been through so much for someone of your age and now you're an adult, you have your own home, you've been decorating and making it look nice and cosy and you're all grown up. To me you'll never stop being a little girl. I will always do what I can to protect you, to help you and be there for you. Family isn't just about blood, it's about those deep connections with those that we choose to be a part of our family too. You will always be part of my family no matter what.

We love you lots
Vicky Robinson – your ever-loving ex step mum and family – your family xxx

Dear baby, the one who left their footprints on my heart,

I never met you, but sometimes I feel like I can hear you calling out to me whenever I'm alone. I carried you inside of me, only for a few months, but I didn't feel like you ever left. Sometimes I feel your feet kick me when I'm in the bath, my stomach flutters, just like those new feelings of movement when baby starts to be felt.

I will never forget the day I lost you, I had been eating Quorn pieces with rice, trying to be healthy for my growing baby. I started feeling pains like those of menstrual cramping. I went to the bathroom and that's when I saw the blood. I had never been pregnant before, but I knew that I was losing you. I cried and cried but I couldn't accept it.

We called 111 and an emergency doctor eventually called back. The words he said to me will haunt me forever, "just lay down and rest, it's God's way". I felt the anger rise within me, what was he trying to say? That God was the reason for my baby's death?

I still wasn't happy, we decided to go to Accident and Emergency, which was probably the wrong thing to do looking back, but I honestly felt like someone somewhere could do something to save you. This couldn't be the end. I was treated like I was a robot, with no feelings at all. I was given an enormous pad and told to do a pregnancy test in the toilet. It came back negative. I was told to go home and rest.

What did these people not understand, how could I go home and rest? Rest was for people who wanted to relax, not someone who had just lost their child. There was no kindness in any of the health professional's words. Weren't they meant to be a caring profession?

We went home and I cried like I've never cried before. A few days later I received a letter through the post. The letter was an appointment to come for my 12-week scan. This felt like a personal attack on me. They knew I had lost my baby; they knew because I was there, in that hospital, crying, holding my stomach and feeling like nobody cared. Of course, I knew it was an automatic letter, sent out in advance, but at that time, it certainly didn't feel that way. I remember it was raining, all I could think to do was go outside in the garden and let the rain mix in with my tears. Maybe it would end like Alice in Wonderland, where she cried so much so ended up floating off in her own stream of tears.

We went to see the GP and it was the first bit of kindness I had felt from a professional. He explained miscarriages and didn't treat me like I was being silly for grieving for my unborn, undeveloped embryo. As much as he couldn't help me to feel better, I did at least have some hope for the future. I could never replace you, but at least I felt like I could try again, when it felt right.

Your birthday would have been in November and I always wondered whether you would have been born on your Grandad's birthday. November has always remained a strange month. I was to marry my second husband on your Grandad's birthday in November, but it was also the same month we lost your Great Grandad, my best friend Ina, and my other best friend's husband.

I think about you all of the time, but every November my body seems to know. I feel an immense sadness and emptiness that permeates my entire being.

I still feel your soul inside of me, and that gives me peace.

I love you baby.
Mummy xxx

15.

Leigh Barnard

To my beautiful Ava

It is February 2021, and you are 8 years old. I am writing you this letter so that in many years to come you will know just how much you are loved and cared for. You are my 3rd born child and you were a very wanted late addition to my life. You have a gorgeous older sister and a funny, crazy big brother, you are the youngest by twenty-two years.

You came into my life when I was forty-two years old all 9lb 1oz of you. You were beautiful, over the first years you brought me so much joy and when you walked at 10 months old, I knew you were trouble.

Fast forward to now and you are a sassy, funny, energetic, clever young lady. You try your very best and you always make people smile and laugh. At the moment you are driving me crazy with your dancing and your latest ambition to be a contortionist.

We have the most amazing conversations, and I am amazed at the knowledge you have. No matter how grown up you are you still like a cuddle and you are always saying Mumma I love you.

Well, I love you more.

I hope we have lots and lots of time to do so many things together. On a more serious note, all that matters to me is your happiness and doing as much as we can together. Traveling, going shopping and making special memories. Family is so very important. I will be proud of you no matter what you choose to do in life as long as it makes you happy.

Your brother and sister will always be there for you and even though your sister wanted to be the only girl she soon come round when she saw you.

Always dream big, never regret and don't let anyone ever change you because you are unique.

My ultimate dream is to see you and your sister and brother happy and treated like the special people you are.

At the moment you are making memories with Nanny and you have a special bond even though you both like to annoy one another, and it drives me crazy. You're as bad as each other but every night you run up to Nanny's room and pull her bed clothes back and put all her things next to her bed. It makes me so proud.

You still hold a special place in your heart for Nanny Rosie and your grandads who are no longer with us. You never forget them and talk about them often. Your heart is bigger than the universe, always keep it that way. It may get bruised at times but let this make you stronger, don't ever give it away and only give it to those who deserve it.

I write this letter from the heart with all the love in the world.

All my love
Mumma xxxxx

Dedicated – To all my family and friends with love xx

16.

Naomi Eskowitz

You Are Enough...

Long before I even thought of you, I knew that one day I would become a Mother. And let me say before I begin, that I love you all more than anything else in the whole world.

I learnt at a young age the values and morals that were important in being able to parent, and more than that I learnt vital skills from my own Mother, Barbara, your Grandma who we sadly lost back in 2013 to MND. She left a huge place in my heart, but you have all helped me to fill that hole, just a little bit.

I had a happy childhood, playing with friends and making news ones. I was quite academic and enjoyed school, both the learning parts and gaining social skills that would set me off on my own journey into becoming your Mummy.

Barbara was a good teacher, kind but firm, the perfect combination to mould me into the woman

I am today and along with my two older Brothers and my Dad we, like every family had our ups and downs but ultimately, we knew that we were loved. I often say that if I could be half of the Mother that she was to me then I am doing a good job and I do not think she will be disappointed!

When I met your Daddy, Stephen, we instantly became good friends, but it took a long time for that friendship to flourish. We were working at the same company for many years, and I often joke that we found love in a hopeless place! Thanks Rhianna…

I remember our first day out as a family of four, Sammie you were 6 and I think Louie you were nearly 4 and I was introduced to you as Daddy's friend, which at the time was true. That day will stay with me for the rest of my life, little Louie in his Thomas the Tank Engine t-shirt and Sammie in his Lego one, we had lots of fun and got to stroke some fish at the Blue Planet Aquarium, a place that we have visited several times since.

Fast forward to today you have both shown great resilience through what has been a terrible year. Sammie you are now 16 and looking forward to the rest of your life, I want to remind you that you are enough. You are loved, and you are growing into a handsome, thoughtful, kind, and intelligent young man. Things may be tough right now but remember you have survived 100% of the toughest moments in your life so far and so I know you will be okay. Louie I am not quite sure when it happened but for a few years now I have been in awe of the human that you are. You face life head on with such gusto and empathy, you are my Superhero and I love you. Just keep on being yourself Son, as you are a marvellous specimen of a person and for that I thank you! You are an amazing artist, and I am mesmerised by your knowledge of Roller Coasters. I really do hope that you get to live out your dream of working in Alton Towers one day!

Jorja, my first born and our Princess, I could not think of anyone I would rather argue with daily; it is like talking to myself. You are growing up to be a beautiful, strong and intelligent young lady and I love you. My life changed drastically when you came along and for the better as you gave me a reason to carry on after I lost Grandma when I was pregnant with you. You are sassy, silly, independent and creative, you are charming, confident, and determined. Not a day goes by that I am not flabbergasted by your use of the English language and I adore your desire to read every book and magazine that crosses your path. Keep being yourself Baby Girl as Mummy is so very proud of you.

To Jessie, my little girl who was too beautiful to grace this world. I hope that you are looking after Grandma up there in the clouds and please make sure she doesn't spend all her heavenly pennies at Bingo! One day we will meet again, and I will get to finally give you the cuddles which I have missed so dearly…

And finally, to Zia my little warrior and rainbow baby. The beautiful boy with the long curly hair and big hazel-coloured eyes. You healed Mummy's soul and helped her to carry on being a Mummy. I know that eventually I will miss the days that I am constantly tidying up your toys and picking up lolly sticks so, for now, just you be you, and please remember never to stop giving Mummy those epic cuddles as I am not sure how I will cope if you stop giving them to me twenty times a day!

Please remind me to smile more, hug you more, say I love you more, tickle, and laugh, and even cry with joy. Please help me be the Mummy that you all deserve.

Please do not be angry or frustrated at the world, I will tell you all once again that you need to not worry about things that are not within your control, life is for living and this is no rehearsal, each day is a brand-new show. No repeat, no rewind. So, give it your best shot in all your worthy acts as the show must go on and on...

And if I had to choose between loving you and breathing. Then I would use my last breath to tell you that I love you...

Love You More!
Mummy
X

17.

Sami Speakman

That's Just Flynn

Flynn, my amazing boy!

The world is upside down and life, at the moment, has been a bit of a struggle for everyone because, whilst I write this, we are in the middle of the Covid 19 pandemic. You have missed so much school last year and this year due to it not being safe, but you have taken it all in your stride, completed all of your work and even started a new school. That I must admit, I was very worried about. Not for me…but for you.

In March 2019 you left school, the school you had been in since you were 3 and a half. The school where all your friends were, an environment where normality and familiarity were a comfort to you. But all that got taken away….. Class work became homework, you couldn't see your friends or family and we were in the middle of a house move.

We moved to a new house in August 2020. This meant a new school, new friends and an environment that was unfamiliar. All this was a big worry because we know how much of a worrier you are. But you surprised us all…

On the first day of your new school, you walked in, leaving daddy and I behind because we couldn't come in with you. Not going to lie, that was horrible. I knew how much you were going to worry and get upset because you didn't know where to go, who all these new faces were, who your teacher is and what the routine of the classroom was. Is your teacher going to know and understand that you can get emotional when you are scared of the unknown? Or will she ignore you?

But Flynn, you smashed it! You stood tall, didn't give up, took it in your stride and you appeared at the end of the day with a big smile on your face!

As much as you wear your heart on your sleeve, let emotions get in the way and get upset at the first sign of the unknown, you have to remember not to beat yourself up, overcome them and try your hardest. YOU HAVE GOT THIS!

We all make new mistakes, every day. We all have to try new things to figure out what we are good at. Sometimes it's scary, but we don't learn without getting it wrong.

But look how far you have come….

We have always been on adventures together and I love seeing you grow. I get little snippets of how you are going to be when you are older, and I can't wait to see what kind of man you become. If this is what you will be like when you are older, then you are going to be amazing!

But much as you deal with your emotions behind the scenes, you have always jumped into things feet first…my little adrenaline junkie. You are one of the only people I know who will go up to the glass floor in Blackpool tower and jump right on it!

You have achieved so much for a young age and both daddy and I are super proud of how kind-hearted you are, how much of a big heart you have, a sense for adventure and the caring nature you have for those around you and the animals you see – no wonder animals love you so much!

We are so proud of how many 5k runs you have completed to raise money for those in need and those who are poorly. But for you it has never been about the medal that is given to you at the end, it's always been 'I want to help mummy'. You have even tackled a few 10k runs to keep training, not many 8-year-olds could do that. You should be proud of yourself, because we all are.

You are currently a yellow belt in karate, due to grade for your next belt. Even though some of the moves do confuse you, you overcome it, push forward and train really hard. That's amazing!

Over the years we have noticed how much you love music; well, it was a given seeing as your first gig was in my tummy and you danced the night away! From then on, we knew you would have some love for music, we didn't know just how much. Music used to stop you mid cry – the healing powers of music!

This love for music is one of my favourite qualities you have. It doesn't matter what mood either of us are in, play a song (and play it loud for the whole world to hear) and we dance like no one is watching and dance all our troubles away...together. I hope you keep hold of that when you are older and keep growing the love for music.

When I look at you, I see myself looking back at me. It's like a little piece of my heart is out there running around being the best they can be.

If you are reading this for the first time or millionth time, at whatever age you are. We want you to remember a few things....

I want you to know we are always with you.
Don't give up, don't give in.
We will always be there when you need us.
You know who are.
Never change for anyone. If someone can't like or love you for who you are, then they are not for you, No one should make you cry and if they do... walk away.

When you stand tall, you are unbreakable.

I love you 3000

Always, All my love
Mummy and Daddy
XXXX

Dedication: To my very own Superhero, Flynn. I love you 3000

18.

Nicola R

To my Darling Children

You are the most precious things in the world to me. The days you entered into my world altered my life in ways I could never have begun to imagine.

You brought a totally new perspective and meaning to my life. I protected you both with every ounce of my life. Many times, I put you both before myself. I often put myself right at the bottom of that all-important chore list, that seemed never ending at times.

Wake you – Check
Feed you - Check
Get you to school – Check
Get home – erm… Rest, Work, and at some point In the afternoon I will remember to take my morning medications.
Get you home from school – Check.

I never envisioned family life being both your mum and dad. When you were both born, your Dad and I were still married, I believed we were happy. Until one day he decided he wasn't happy anymore.

It broke me, but you were both still young. I don't know how much you remember the tears and the heartbreak I went through. I blamed myself for him leaving. I tried so hard to be the loving mother, wife, daughter I eventually realised I had no idea who I was. I was a blank – who would love someone who had no-idea who they were. I had moulded myself to fit into everyone else's expectations I lost all essence of me.

If I have taught you anything in life; you will know how fiercely I defend the need to be you. Unapologetically you! Be Kind, Have Courage but always be you!

Despite your Dad and I being separated, he is still a big part of your life, and although I still find it hard at times. I will always be grateful that you are both loved by an endless flow of family and friends who support us on both sides.

You might also recall a time I remarried; they say in life you get second chances. I believed he was the one; but in reality, I'd been drawn into his world of false promises and illusion. It didn't take long for the wolf to emerge and I'm so very glad it all happened when it did.

I wasn't able to tell you all the details at the time as there were a lot of words about that you wouldn't fully understand for many years. The social workers that assessed you were pleased that he hadn't done anything untoward with you. But truth be told he was a horrid creature – commonly known as a paedophile. He didn't go to jail, but he was stopped from making contact with us. I divorced him as quickly as I could, and deed polled my name to match yours again. Although I'm no longer married to your Dad, it made sense to keep that name.

I never thought I would be divorced twice before turning 40, but honestly, it's looking after you that gives me the strength and courage to keep going.

Watching the two of you grow up together as brother and sister can be trying at times as you, daughter, can be a bit of a drama Queen. But you both give me pride and purpose.

I sit here at my desk writing this letter to you. Looking around me and recalling my day. Home-schooling has just ended and schools go back next week. You both helped me tidy the house without any prompts. It made me smile, as you both know my energy levels are suffering at the moment. Although we'd had some animated arguments today, you both gave me some amazing hugs and were excited when your new books arrived.

I feel honoured that you have both inherited my joy of reading. You both sink yourselves into books at bedtime, and I don't insist that you do. It's your choice and I did the same at your age too. You are both aspiring authors as well, which you might not think much of at times but really, it's an impressive feat. You both make me so proud and watching you grow day by day into amazing people brings joy to me.

You both often quiz why I do what I do for work. But you know my answer will always be the same. Having my own business allows me to do things on my terms. If you are ill – I take the day off. If I am ill, I can rest. If we are in lockdown then I spin many plates to try and achieve whatever I can on any given day. Why? So that I can raise and support my children the best way I know how. My Way. Now I'm not going to say I'm some kind of super mum. But I didn't have children for someone else to raise them for me, nor do I have the good fortune of having the ability to juggle a 'proper' job whist managing my health issues. I tried that when you my lovely boy was tiny. It created so much stress and anxiety within me I couldn't bear the thought of trying to do the same with two children. So, running my own business was for me the only option and who knew I would be this good at it!

I know you are both proud of me, you've said it to me many times now and it makes my whole body smile inside and out. When you recognise such profound things around you it makes me look at you both and think rather proudly to myself. If I do nothing else well in this life, I know I am raising two amazing, beautiful humans.

My Love Always

Our Queen

Inside every daughter born lies the eggs of her granddaughter
The seed of the flower yet to be planted
A whole generation away

Bonds sown before life created
Intended to be fruitful before life is expired.
Your Life was so precious
As is those that followed in your footsteps as we laid
you to rest
As you look down upon us
We know you're our angel, and simply the best!
80 was young for you
Still life of the party
Still playing cards for money
Fancy Dress was a speciality
Widowed twice but still going
Never single for long
Tina Turner – Simply the Best!
Will Always be your Song!

A Poem to a Grandmother taken cruelly and suddenly
by Covid 19 just before Christmas 2020. She was
Mother to 4, Grandmother to 9 and Great Grandma
or GG to more than fingers and almost toes.

From The Best Mistake You Ever Made,

This was how I knew myself to be justified as I grew
up, only child to a teen Mum & Dad, to be shortly
hit with the bereavement of your own father.

I know this hit everyone really hard.

I was a baby at the time, but it wasn't until Grandma's funeral that I realised just how much my presence at the time had impacted on everyone.

You were the eldest of 4, all your sisters and brother were also teens and your mum was now a widow, depending on you to help. Me, I was just the baby, the one that distracted everyone with the good life could bring back to the world. The one that reminded everyone that there was a life worth living.

I can't say that my arrival was divine intervention, or anything like that but I'm a great believer in things happening for a reason.

I know you still reflect back on your Dad, and wish you had chance to say some things you never got chance to say. I know you were happy that he got to meet a grandchild. I know how much he adored me. The smile on his face in the old pictures says it all.

The reason I'm writing this is that you worry too much about the past, when my brother came along.

Yeah, I was a twit. And granted I've made mistakes. But who doesn't!

But what I do want you to know is that even though you were a teen mum – all of my school mates loved YOU! They would have swapped you for their mum in a heartbeat.

In their eyes their parents were far too strict, whereas me and you – we're Soul Sisters, you can read me like a book. We call each other often at the same time and wonder why we can't get through. I can talk to you about anything and we support each other always!!

There have been times where I know you've found it difficult, and I've found it hard as sometimes and I've needed to act like the parent to help you. But we both have the strength and the courage to see anything through!

I think sometimes I see so much of myself in you its rather scary. I know I don't have the life you had hoped for me. But in many ways what I do have is so much better and much more authentic and wholesome.

You know the children love you, and so do I.

So Remember
Love You Always xxx

Dedicated to those in my past, present and future

19.

Sue Clegg

My Beautiful Miracles

Amelia Grace, we never even got to meet you! We wanted you so badly! We found out we would struggle to have you, so we turned to the support of a fertility clinic early on. They put me on fertility drugs to begin with to see if we could get pregnant that way. Amazingly 18 months down the line we got pregnant with you! Daddy and I were soooooo excited! All we wanted was you. We even had your name picked out for if you were a girl – to us you will always be Amelia Grace.

Mummy's birthday came and we checked that we could fly to Dublin for the weekend, just me, daddy and our little miracle inside me. They said it was fine, so we did. All weekend I was so tired and drained but that was OK because you were inside me.

The day after we got back, we had an appointment for a scan at the clinic. We weren't even worried about it so when the midwife said there was no heartbeat it was like a bolt of lightning striking us both. All I could do was cling to your daddy and say sorry over and over again. I felt it was my fault. We shouldn't have gone away. I should have rested, and you would still be here. I know now that you were made to be an angel but even now it hurts that we didn't get to meet you.

Our world fell apart – but I didn't actually lose you. Instead, I had to carry your lifeless body inside of me for a week and then I had to go through the most horrific labour (even though I had only been 9 weeks pregnant). Everything about that awful day will stay with me forever. Your daddy never left my side all the way through. In an odd way it brought us even closer together.

So darling girl, we never actually got to meet you, not in the way we wanted, but you did bring mummy and daddy even closer together. Maybe that was your purpose so that we would be strong enough to have your little sister.

All my love
Mummy xxxx

Louisa Elizabeth, you are our second miracle! You were our IVF rainbow baby. One day we will tell you all about how you came about and how you were so wanted, how you might have had a sibling but sadly it just wasn't meant to be. No matter what you do we will always be grateful for you in our lives.

Whilst I was pregnant both daddy and I spent our time worried about losing you. I wrote you letters as you grew and started to move about because I was so scared that I may never get to tell you how precious you were and that you are our miracle.

Deep in our hearts daddy and I wanted a little girl but we were so scared that at scans and check-ups all we wanted to know was that you were safe and healthy. You were so strong and would spend your time dancing in my tummy. We nicknamed you Bumpy because you bumped about in my tummy (Daddy still calls you his Bumpy Baby). You knew when daddy was close and would wake up and kick him. You already had that close relationship with him that continues now. I loved how his face would light up to watch you moving.

You made a dramatic entrance into our lives and even now you love to be a drama queen. But you are our drama queen, and we are so proud of you!

As you grow up, I hope we teach you all the values that will help you to get through your life. You are already independent and sassy. I hope you remain that way. I hope you remember to be thoughtful and think before you speak. Your words can wound if you are careless with them and sometimes those wounds can run deep. I hope you are never at the end of someone else's wounding words or actions.

You will have hard times to go through, that's just how life is but know beautiful girl that daddy and I will always be here for you no matter what you do or what life throws at you. We will support and guide you in the best way we can, but we will always encourage you to find your way. No-one else's way, just your way.

I hope you aren't easily led and remain the confident girl you are.

My advice when you are unsure of anything is to stop, breath and think. What would gran do? What would mummy or daddy do? Hopefully that will guide you. At the end of the day Bumpy, don't do anything that puts you in danger or means you will die!!! And don't be an idiot or do anything that is idiotic!

Be thoughtful and kind and the wonderful little girl I know you are! I look forward to walking by your side as you grow and being your mummy to guide you where I can. Gran has taught me well and she did a great job with me so hopefully I can do the same for you.

I love you with all my heart and I always will.
All my Love now and forever
Mummy xxxx

20.

Gemma Walkden

To My Little Warrior and Queen, That Made Me A Mummy

To my Daisy,

I hope you know just how much I love you and how proud you make me every single day. Sometimes I can't believe that you are my daughter and that you are nearly 3 and a half. I am so lucky to be your Mummy.

You recently started nursery and you have taken it all in your stride. I was full of worries and concerns about how you would be. You see, this past year has been a really strange one for us. We haven't been able to go out to a lot of our usual favourite places. We went months without seeing family and friends too. It broke my heart when you would ask to go to a particular place or to see one of your favourite people and I had to say no. I was worried you would struggle in a new place with new people because of this. But even when you told me on your first full day of nursery that you were feeling a bit nervous, you walked straight in. You have got stuck into nursery life and have made friends. You run out of nursery covered in mud, paint and whatever else you have played with that day. You have the biggest smile on your face and give me the biggest hug.

I absolutely adore the person you are and are becoming. You are a little lady who knows exactly what you want. I hope you are always this strong willed and don't let others opinions sway you. We need more people like you in the world.

I love our time together and the adventures we go on, the books we read, the songs we sing and the play dates we go on. You love being round people like your Mummy and it is wonderful to watch you with your little friends. You are kind, caring, funny, happy and confident and just an absolute joy to be around.

As your Mummy, I worry about what the world will be like as you get older. There seem to be different challenges and more pressure in the world compared to when I was young. I hope that you know I will always be there for you whether that be a listening ear or cheering you on. You can do anything you want to do Daisy, I just want you to be happy.

Daisy, I hope you continue to be your amazing self as you get older. I can't wait to see what new adventures we get up to.

Love you to the moon and back.
All My Love Mummy xxx

21.

Melanie Broughton

To My Very Own Superhero and other ADHD Superheros Everywhere

My Darling Son,

This is without a doubt the hardest thing I have ever had to write. What do I say to the most important person in my universe? How do I do you justice? Yet, I think it's essential that I write this, no matter how hard this is to do. There are things I want to say to you that I think might get lost in a conversation. I believe you would benefit from having something in writing; something permanent that you can keep and read whenever you need to. If we chat about this, I'm afraid we'd both get far too easily distracted onto other subjects.

So, here is my letter to you with some key things I really want you to know, some wonderful memories and hopefully, some solid advice for the future.

It breaks my heart when you look at me with those beautiful hazel eyes and ask with such sincerity, "Mum, is it just ADHD that's wrong with me?" Let's

172

get something straight – there is nothing wrong with you. What is wrong is the actual perception you have of ADHD. Maybe that's our fault. Maybe, in the early days of pre-diagnosis when we didn't know the reasons for your meltdowns, when every waking hour seemed chaotic and fractious, when mainstream school had washed their hands of you, when you regularly inflicted pain on those around you and self-harmed, when ornaments and furniture were destroyed, entire rooms turned upside down, when there was deprivation of sleep and we were completely exhausted and knew no better, then yes, your dad and I asked "what is wrong with him?"

We are incredibly lucky. Your father and I were able to fight for support. Having a diagnosis meant so much more than knowing the name of your condition and getting you medicated. We have been able to research the condition and we are better equipped to support you now. Things aren't perfect; I don't ever think they will be, but things are much more manageable now.

But you do still have dark days. You suffer also from insomnia and anxiety, and you still think there is something wrong with you. For these reasons, I want you to keep this letter close by at all times.

Everybody has a hero. A few days before World Book Day, I listened to you on your English Zoom lesson talking about heroes. My heart filled when you told your teacher that your dad and I are your heroes. You are not our hero. No. You are our superhero. You see, superheroes have superpowers. And boy, do you have superpowers! Peter Parker got bitten by a spider and became Spiderman, Bruce Banner became The Hulk after being exposed to gamma radiation, Tony Stark built himself a metallic suit filled with technology to become Iron Man, but you were born with special powers! Powers which, when used properly, can help you to achieve anything you want to in life. I want you to recognise your superpowers and celebrate them. I want you to realise how special you really are.

Your first superpower is thinking outside of the box. Your ADHD lets you think differently, which means you find unique solutions to tricky situations that other people might miss. You're an expert in problem solving. You don't always find the most conventional solution, but they are solutions nevertheless. Like the time when you had just turned four, and at nursery one day you spotted a rather large spider scurrying across the floor. You knew that Heather*, your key worker, was petrified of these creepy crawlies and there would be uproar. You instantly threw a pot of blue paint across the room, creating a mess and diversion before stamping on the classroom intruder. Yes, you got in trouble, but there was no screaming – at least not from Heather. I am not telling you to hurl paint to resolve issues, but don't be afraid to see problems as challenges you can overcome by thinking differently. Many years ago, a young man with ADHD was stranded in a tiny airport on an island with hundreds of other passengers when his plane got cancelled. Instead of waiting for an unknown length of time for a new flight, he got on the phone and chartered a flight. He couldn't afford it, so he divided the cost of the plane by the number of seats and charged every passenger $39, covering the cost of the plane and resolving the issue for everybody. That young man was Richard Branson, future founder of Virgin Atlantic airlines. You see, his ADHD superpower led to the beginning of a multi-million-pound company.

Don't let anyone tell you that your ADHD means you can't concentrate. On the contrary, you have a power called Hyperfocus. When you are really interested in something, you can focus on what you are doing for many hours after most neurotypical people have given up. On Christmas Day 2020, you built three Lego robots designed for adults in under three hours. You're just twelve. Last Summer, you managed to dig up a small, troublesome tree in our back garden. You were at it almost all day. I had given up after about twenty minutes, but not you – you even got your little spade out and chipped away at the soil, bit by bit, until you were able to free it from the ground.

Thanks to this superpower, many people like you with ADHD have been very successful. Some of the greatest minds and inventors are thought to have had ADHD. Graham Bell, Isaac Newton and Thomas Edison are proof that living with ADHD is no hindrance that 'lightbulb moment'. Right now, you want to be a zookeeper. You'll be a brilliant zookeeper. You just need to tune in to your hyperfocus power when you need it and you can do anything.

Your compassion is another superpower. Most children have compassion, but those with ADHD often show more than most. Your compassion has already done amazing things. This superpower also first became apparent at nursery. You were three and befriended a little girl called Mia★. You had been there for two years at that time, but Mia had only started a few days earlier. According to Heather, you noticed that she was stood in a corner, alone and looking uncertain. Without hesitation, you walked over to her, said hello and held her hand as you led her to the sand table. You played, albeit silently, which was most unusual for you. Heather couldn't keep her eyes off the both of you the whole time, but your silence was not the reason for Heather's amazement. No, Mia was talking, quite animatedly in fact. You see, Mia had selective mutism. The simplest way of explaining it is somebody who might be chatty in their own home but cannot say a word in certain situations and places. In Mia's case, she had never spoken to anybody outside her own family before. This was a life-changer. How amazing. By showing kindness, you got her talking, and nobody knows how important it is to talk more than you.

Memory is both your superpower and your kryptonite. I have lost count of the number of times I have to tell you to go upstairs and fetch a pair of socks, only for you to wander back downstairs, bare-footed, waving a piece of Lego or a Star Wars toy in your hand instead. I'll send you back up again and you'll come down with a poke ball, or something else just not sock-related. Yet, you can reel off names of individual Dr. Who episodes – including those aired before even I was born. Or you'll compile one of your infamous lists of endless things, such as car models as you see them, and you won't need to refer back to it to check which ones you have or haven't seen, even when your list has over fifty items on it.

Yes, your ADHD does cause issues, but you should never underestimate the benefits it can bring. You are creative, never boring. You get bored often, but not for long as you find something else to do very quickly. You are curious. VERY curious, so this means you are able to learn at superspeed about the things that interest you. This is why it is so important to really think about which subjects you enjoy at school as it also gives you the potential to do exactly what you want to do in adulthood. You really can be what you want to be - except invisible. I'm so sorry to break this news to you but covering up your eyes doesn't mean we can't see you. We can!

Unfortunately, it does mean that working on the things you don't want to do is much harder for you. And it has to be done. There's no magic formula but know this: your dad and I will be there for you every step of the way. There is no reason why you cannot go to university, but equally, your dad and I will be just as happy if you choose something more vocational. We only ask that you do your best and that you are happy and know that you are loved.

Spiderman once said, "With great power comes great responsibility!" He was so right. You will have to reign in some of your powers just to stop things from spiralling out of control and to keep out of trouble. Just like The Hulk, you too become very strong and destructive when you get frustrated and angry. It has taken three adults to hold you down before now.

Controlling your emotions might seem like a mountainous task at the moment, but it will get easier with time. You have to work on the various strategies we have taught you and remember to take your medication to stop your powers from getting out of control. Sadly, you will have to accept that many people still do not understand ADHD powers. You will learn, with our help and unfailing support, to use your superpower of compassion towards those people, and together we will find a way to help you explain ADHD in your own words and maybe also help others with ADHD to recognise their own superpowers.

Your dad and I are incredibly proud of our amazing superhero!

All my Love,
Mum x

*names have been changed.

22.

Colleen Higgins

To The Ones That Bring Me Joy And Happiness Even On The Dark Days

Dear Trin

My dear you have grown so much since I first met you when you were 10 and now you are 17. Things were so different back then, we just played. I don't know when that changed, it probably wasn't too long in since I have difficulty keeping my mouth shut. I wanted to be part of your life and be someone to you and I guess I tried to be the stepmother because that was the only role that seemed to be appropriate for us. That seemed to be when I started to take an active role in the family and not just date your father but think of us as a family. Ever since then I became the disciplinarian and the one to help you with your homework instead of being just your father's girlfriend.

Each year became harder to help you with your homework, not just because the work demanded more but you became less willing to do it. I don't know why I care so much about homework; it is your life to screw up, but I feel like I need to stop you from possibly ruining your life. I look ahead, I know the consequences of failing or just dropping out; you can't get a job nowadays without at least a high school education.

Each year has gotten worse, like last week me having to write that paper for you on Lord of the Flies because you couldn't be bothered to read a damn book. I just don't get it. You have nothing else to do, no job, no chores, no responsibility at all. Just being a student and you won't even do that. I don't know why I do your homework or allow this to be our situation, but it is ruining us and me.

Lately it has been so hard to talk to you without getting angry and stressed, I guess this is because it seems like I care more about your future than you do. This has been our norm for a while though. Each year has not just become harder, but it has been more tense between us, with more resentment because we both feel like the other person doesn't understand. I feel that you don't care, about much really. Except your boyfriend, and yes, I remember those days, which makes me want to apologize to my mother daily. It is lie after lie with you, omission and constant manipulation of most stories that come out of your mouth.

You don't even say thank you, I am just expected to help with homework, buy you whatever you want. I look forward to summer, not just the weather but the fact that there is no school. We can be carefree and laugh without me walking through the door and asking about homework that is only done here and never at your mother's. We need to cram a year's worth of fun into the summers to make up for the rest of the year. We have so much fun swimming and now that your sister is older camping will be awesome.

Thank you for helping with her, you are such a great sister. We just need to get through these next couple of years with school and we will be fine. You will be done with papers and I will be done with homework! We can do this!

Honestly, I am willing to be the bitch that I am so often called by both you and your father, if it will get you a diploma. I will be whatever I need to be. I just hope at some time down the road we can get over this and you will understand why I did this for you. I care about you and your future.

I am not the cuddly affectionate type, maybe that is why we are confused about where we stand with each other. I tried to tell you how I feel about you, how much I love and care about you, but you didn't respond, so I dropped it. I show my love by caring about you and helping you since you don't seem to know what to do with my words. I do love you; you are not from my body but I chose you.

All My Love your Bitchy Stepmother

Dear Eliza,

No matter what else happens in my life you are my crowning achievement. That might sound silly or glorifying you but it's true. You have changed me in so many ways. I never thought of myself as a motherly individual, let alone affectionate in a way that I thought a mother should be. I might not be the overly affectionate and touchy mother, but I love our cuddle time. The sleeping with you kind of sucks, not going to lie. What happened? You used to sleep so well by yourself, now we don't even last a few minutes before you come and get me, telling me that you are scared. You never are able to explain what you are actually afraid of, maybe you just need that contact. Sometimes I need that too, so that I feel grounded and a part of the world when things are too much to handle.

It is okay, we will work through it, together, if you need me.

They were not wrong when they said that once you start talking, you will never stop, after fighting for a year and a half to get you speech therapy I am so happy to say that you are able to communicate. Not just communicate like we used to, where you would point or gesture or coax me into understanding you without words but talking. For such a little one and having had trouble speaking your grasp on humour astounds me. I wish you were still in speech therapy but after only a year and a few months they found you to be reaching age-appropriate speech norms. I just know how much you prospered with it, how many leaps and bounds you made with your education too.

You are so smart; I can't believe how you soak up all that information and keep it. You are really interested in space, everything from planets to the stars. We look at Orion every night, you find his belt. I think for the first time since we have been looking for it you found Taurus, well the eye, the rest is mostly behind the trees. When it is a little warmer, I think this next week will even be warmer at night, we can go out before bed and find the big dipper. Looking at the stars or looking up constellations before bed has become our thing right now.

I need to read you a story before bed, I feel like I am always slacking on my motherly duties and never doing enough for you. I do homework with your sister and leave you to play on the tablet, I should spend more time playing with you instead of reading or playing on my own tablet. I am just so stressed right now, and you are paying the price. I really need to start putting you to bed earlier too, you are my night owl just like me. Your tendency to wake up early eludes me though, that is more like Auntie, she wakes up early. Hindsight is always 20/20 they say, I know what I should do to be a better and more involved mother, I hope that I can actually live up to my own standards.

I want you to stay strong, though the attitude I can do without, but the sass makes you who you are. My little spitfire! So, keep the attitude and the silly craziness that is you. I love you bunches. Always remember that. Don't let anyone take that light out of you, there is a special essence to you, like a presence. When you are not here the house feels empty, I know, I know but it is the truth. You are something special my dear. You are a beautiful soul, keep that light.

All My Love, your awed and amused Mom

23.

Hollie Ann

My Reason To Be Better & Achieve The Impossible

To my reason why… Squiggle, Squigglish, Chewbacka

Let's go back to the start…. Me and dad had many discussions about having children and how many we wanted. One day he told me he had fertility issues and how it would affect our chances of conceiving naturally. We came to the agreement we would try to have our own baby and if we could not, we would adopt. That was fine by both of us, but I knew I really wanted to be able to carry my baby in my tummy. I would not want to miss scans, feeling sick, the kicks, sitting in my ribs, needing to pee all the time and cravings, but most of all experiencing the euphoric feeling of pushing my baby out of my vagina. The instant love you feel for this tiny, weird alien looking baby you have been handed. Like a scene from the lion king but looking at your partner with that euphoric look of love in your eyes and just knowing this was what we waited for.

This is where your story begins…. I knew before you were a little embryo in my uterus, that you would be a boy, so I brought you a blue star vest and a grey one too as I just knew in my heart, I would be having a boy. It took us 4-6 months to make you, which the doctor said was really good.

On the 26th of April 2013 I said to your dad to get a pregnancy test before he went to work because I knew I was pregnant this time, but daddy had to prepare mummy for the 100,000th test could say negative, as mummy wanted you so badly that mummy was testing all the time. As daddy brushed his teeth and mummy was on the toilet, mum took the test and placed it on the side of the bath. Me and dad patiently waited for the 3 minutes to be up. I sat there on the toilet and daddy kept brushing his teeth. We both looked at each other and I told daddy I was pregnant - we were having a baby. I knew you would be a boy, I could just feel it in my heart, so we had already picked your name. We wanted it to mean something to me and daddy, so we named you after some of the most important men in our lives.

When you were growing in my tummy, it was a magical experience. Feeling you kick me and move around to get comfortable, always ending up on my bladder and making me need to wee all day and all night. The only thing I did not like was you always made me sick when I ate anything with tomato in it – daddy would always say he is definitely my child.

When it came to giving birth to you, mummy, daddy and your fairy godmother were there. I would say it was a hard time for all of us. I started getting the pain in the morning before daddy had to go to work on the 10th of December 2013. Daddy was still asleep so mummy rang nanny Dee Dee to see when I should go to hospital. Nanny Dee Dee said I should go as my contractions were 2 minutes apart.

Everything was going fine at the hospital, mummy trusted the first two midwives and I had to have pain relief as I was listening to my body and kept trying to push you out, but you were not ready to enter the world just yet. The third midwife was not as good as the other two, I had some complications and mummy ended up having a c section. On the 11th of December 2013 at 2.29am you were born. Me and daddy both cried as the nurse brought you over for me to see your little face. We could not believe you were finally here! I could look at you, hold you, watch you sleep, smell you and touch your little hands and feet. Kiss your cheeks, cradle you till you fell asleep in my arms and stare at you so much.

The first three months of your life were the hardest for mummy, I had not healed as quickly as I should have after the c section. Mummy could barely bend, sit, stand, let alone walk long distances. Making caring for you without daddy there very hard but we managed.

I want to tell you a little bit about how mummy felt during this time, so if you experience something like this you know it's ok to come and talk to me. When we brought you home daddy had to do a lot for you, mummy did not have the strength to do it a lot of the time as the pain could be excruciating. I was very emotional, it should have been the happiest time of my life but it was tainted by the sadness of the things I could not do for you, but now when I look at it I was blessed to have experienced this with you. I wanted to breast feed you, but I only managed to get you latched on once, it was the best feeling in the world even for that 10 minutes. I could not change your first nappy, daddy did; it ended up everywhere as he had never changed a nappy before - which was a funny sight from what I can remember.

I could not really bath you, but daddy did everything he could to make that possible for me to do so. The hardest time for me was at night when daddy would not wake up to you crying to give you to me to feed. It would take mummy sometimes up to 15 minutes to get out of the bed to get to you and I had 16 pillows to keep me in an upright position so I could get out the bed easier. I spent nights crying wishing I was better so I could be the best possible mum to you, and I gave it my best with the challenges I faced at the time.

Aside from the challenges we faced together in the early years of your life, you gave me a feeling in my heart I had never felt before. I don't even know how to explain it to you, it's like every emotion wrapped in love, as long as I had your love, I had a reason to wake up every morning - you gave me purpose! I would just sit for hours looking at you awake or sleep, I would think about all the dreams and hopes I have for us as a family and for you as my son. I want to be the best mum I can be to you. I want to be able to support you, so you can come to me and talk about anything and everything. I want to give you traditions like me and daddy had while we grew up, the morals we have and the family values we hold.

I would say I am far from perfect and I am definitely not the best mum in the world in my eyes, but I might be in your eyes. I am going to make a list of things I want to teach you as you grow into an adult.

- You should always put yourself above others as you and your family are all that matters.

- Never let anyone shh you, speak up and express yourself but try not to be rude.

- Your family doesn't have to be blood.

- Family time has to happen every week, this is so important - make memories.

- When you meet your soulmate treat them how you would treat me, with respect and love endlessly. Remember it's a partnership not a you and I.

- Respect is something a person earns; they don't just get it.

- Give yourself the option to any situation in life - you don't have to do anything you don't want to do.

o Try your best at everything you do.

- When you need a hug - hug someone, if you need to cry - find a shoulder.

- Always talk about how you feel to someone if you cannot come to me and your dad.

- Most of all just be you son, don't change for anyone.

These are just a few of the things I hope I teach you as you grow up. Mine and your dad's love for you is unconditional and we will always stand by you and support you. You are never too old for a hug or chat with your parents. Me and your dad will always have a room waiting for you if you ever want to come home when you're older, of course this means at some point you have to leave home to live your life.

I know when you're older and you read this, you'll think we were hard on you and I would say at times we were. But the world we live in today is not as safe as it once was and I have a fear that you will end up in the wrong crowd, as you are very rebellious at the ripe age of 7.

So, let me tell you about our journey together over the years - testing my patience is an understatement! I try to give you multiple chances to make the right choices, but you are so stubborn that you continue to make the bad choices and I'm still not sure where you get it from, most probably me! I feel like you know what the right choice is but you would rather the negative attention from me. I am trying to teach you different ways we can communicate together to make our relationship the best it can be. Aside of this - let me just tell you how PROUD I am of you! You have come so far and are so resilient at such a young age. Together we have been through a lot and things have changed a lot over the last few years.

Let's just acknowledge at the age you are now, which is 7 years old, how amazing you are, you have me in fits of laughter, you are so funny just like your dad! Talking of like your dad, you literally have the same shape nails even toes! You are a mini version of your dad. You have the same drive your dad does - you want to find out about how things work and how they are made plus what could go wrong - this just fascinates me. Watching you learn and find out about things that make you smile like a Cheshire cat. The passion and drive you have at the age of 7 is inspiring, you make mummy want to achieve better for you. When we have conversations about what job you want to do when you're older, you always tell me you want to be like your dad fixing cars and then you say do the jobs I do to - it absolutely makes my heart melt - you are one amazing little lad!

Your enthusiasm to read is something I hope you carry on throughout your life. Reading about all the different things as you do now will keep your brain ticking over, which is what daddy does, that's how he knows so much. You are such a confident reader, I would say better than mummy - I am so proud of you son for always trying your best and not giving up.

I am sure as you grow up there will be a lot more learning for me and you, but one thing I can tell you is you can always count on me to be there for you. I will always have your back son! I will keep your crown straight! I will never be far from you, as you are my baby boy, no matter how old you are! I hope that you can be open with me and your dad, about the different situations you go through. I never want you to feel alone, me and your dad will always be there for you or on the end of a phone. I will guide you the best I can and give you all the knowledge I have, one thing I do know is you will be able to cook some good tasting food. I want you to live the best life you can safely, as being in the adult world isn't always what it seems, so always keep your wits about you.

Love you lots, love you so much it hurts, around the universe and back.

All my love
Mum
Xoxox

24.

Jennifer Royle

Wish upon a seagull

To my 2 precious little souls

Thank you for giving me the biggest gift and privilege of being your mummy. Before you came into my life I never knew how full my heart could become or how much joy two little people could bring. Since your birth you have both been the light of our lives and we have cherished every little moment with you.

There have been some hard times and you have certainly tried our patience with your strong spirits, sharp wits and stubbornness. These traits are not all bad as they will help you to hold your own in a world full of competition. Use those traits to stand out in a crowd, fight for what you want to achieve and be an individual.

As I write this letter the world as we once knew it has been turned on its head. We have gone from being thrilled, excited and nervous about bringing one of you into the world (that's you little legs) to being told to stay shut inside the house away from all our family and friends. It isn't the year we had hoped for and it's brought everyone so much frustration, upset and fear.

Since the day you could talk little lady, you have wished and wished for a baby brother or sister. I felt so guilty because we had to wait such a long time for you to come along and light up our world, I didn't think we would ever be able to have another little one.

At Christmas time you sat on Santa's knee (back when it was allowed) and asked for a baby brother or sister. I hoped he would say "Santa can't really bring things like that" but instead he replied, "I will see what I can do". On Christmas day you were so excited and giddy about opening all your presents and shrieked with glee as you uncovered each treasure hidden inside the mounds of wrapping paper. After the chaos and excitement of the morning you sat on the sofa and sobbed. I thought perhaps you had been a little overwhelmed and so asked why you were so sad. You looked at me with tear filled eyes and wiped your dripping nose with your sleeve whilst sniffling. Santa forgot one of my presents mummy!! Oh dear I replied. Trying to filter through my brain for something I had forgotten, whispering bad mummy quietly inside my head. What was it that he forgot to bring honey... HeHe hasn't brought me a brother or sister like he said he would. The sobs turned into floods of tears but after a cuddle and offer of Christmas chocolate all was well again. You would gaze in awe at any babies or little siblings that your friends had, and it would break my heart. You watched an animated film called Storks where they delivered babies to families from the baby factory, which quickly became your favourite film.

One day we went to visit family in Wales. You were walking by the sea with your cousins and saw a group of rather large seagulls sat squawking on the harbour. At the top of your voice, you screamed "I want a baby in my mummy's tummy please!!" You clearly thought these huge birds were storks or at least the next best thing, I could have let the ground swallow me.

Passers-by chuckled whilst looking for signs of the blushing parents belonging to the child stood conversing with seagulls and demanding they bring her a sibling!

Little did we know that a month or so later you finally got your ultimate wish. We couldn't wait to tell you and of course you were ecstatic and delighted that you were about to have your dream come true. You even hugged me and said sweetly, mummy see dreams really do come true. I want you to remember this story when you're bickering and fighting with your little brother or when you feel that you have to compete for attention. Remember the love you felt when you saw him for the first time and the happiness you felt when your wish had finally come true. You need to stick together and look out for one another. It was love at first sight for both of you and the same when me and daddy met you both too. You are both our dreams come true.

We have always been such a busy family who loved our family time, making memories and going on adventures on the beach, in the woods and trying new things but all that has had to stop.

Our family adventures have been replaced by home school, local walks and garden fun. The person hit hardest by all these restrictions was probably you my feisty little lady and for this I'm so terribly sorry. You were too young to fully understand what was being asked of you but old enough to feel robbed of your freedom and to grieve for the time we spent with family and friends who you missed so much. We all did.

Home school was tough, really tough. Daddy was working in the hospital and even had a stint there himself due to ill health. I had to help you with your schoolwork as well as tend to tiny little legs who was just a baby. You cried that you didn't want me to be your teacher anymore and just wanted me to be mummy again. I wanted so much to be mummy again too I didn't know who I even was anymore. I tried my best to fill our days with fun where I could. We baked, we worked through all of your Rainbows badges together, we played games, we danced in the kitchen. I loved our time together, but it was so, so exhausting. There have been lots of tears, shouting and cross words from all of us but that doesn't mean that we all love each other any less.

I don't want either of you to only remember the stressful times. The times where I sat and secretly cried because it was all just too much to deal with on my own. I want to remember how much I loved you, how we made a fuss over every festival and celebration. Easter, Halloween, Christmas, Chinese New Year, pancake day, bonfire nights. I wanted your childhoods to be filled with so many happy memories, memories that I had wished I had had when I was young. Little legs is growing so fast and he sees how anxious and upset his big sister is and how frustrated and helpless mummy is feeling. I want so much to scoop you up little lady and tell you that everything is going to be fine, you can conquer the world and I will always adore you no matter what comes our way. These lockdowns have really taken their toll. You were always such a lively, confident little girl who loved having adventures but now you're so scared to go out, we have to drag you screaming to get some exercise and the thought of making mistakes at school fills you with dread and you no longer feel like you are good at anything. Just know that I fought for you… I tried my best to build you back up and I will never stop trying. You are going to do great things I just know but you are not expected to be perfect, perfect people do not achieve great things they just fit perfectly into society.

Do not be afraid of not fitting into that slot. Everyone blossoms when their time is right, just keep going and you will find your path. Sometimes we just have to clear away a few weeds and take a couple of wrong turns and that's ok.

Little legs you have been robbed of all the social interactions that you would have had and have missed out on time with family and friends whom I know would have adored you just as much as us. Most of them had to watch you grow on social media and video calls which they say helped brighten up some of their lock down days. You hated masks and would often try and pull mummies off turning it into a game of peek a boo I pray that you have no lasting anxieties towards interaction with people when we are all allowed to return to some kind of normality. It's no wonder that now we can go for longer walks you delight in the freedom of running through the woods, finding sticks and crunching through leaves. I hope we get to make just as many fun memories with you as we did when your sister was little. Be patient with your sister. She adores you so much that it's sometimes a bit smothering. One day this will help you through some tough times embrace it where you can.

It's no secret that mummy's eyes don't work very well and at the moment it's unsure how much or how little I will be able to see in the future.

Know this, even if I can no longer see your beautiful faces fully the memories we make together will always be engraved in my heart. I will remember your smiles and your frowns, your dimples and your scrunched up noses and they are safely stored in my memory for me to refer to when I need them.

Everything I strive for, every struggle and every achievement has you both in mind. I want to make you strong and resilient, but I also want you to experience everything the world has to offer. If sometimes it feels like we are being too harsh or unreasonable please remember that we are trying to equip you for a world of unfairness and disappointment and as much as we would love to be your bestest friends we have the job of being your parents, your guides, your referees, your cheerleaders and your role models. It's the toughest job in the world but it is also the greatest.

You are both the most precious gifts and were well worth the struggles and long wait. Life won't always be easy and there will be times that you feel like giving up and questioning your worth. These times will pass, you will overcome barriers, you will fight, and you will win. Have faith, have patience and love yourself because we will always have faith in you and love you.

Forever in my heart and soul.
Love mum xx

Dedicated – To my two little miracles, you were well worth the struggles and the wait

25.

Erin James

Dear Beautiful Soul

You are not my stepdaughter. You are my daughter, who just happened to be born before I met you.

I failed a lot during those 7 years that I was with your dad... I don't know if you call him that now, since he has abandoned all aspects of being a dad to you. I usually refer to him as Fuckface... but maybe that's not the most appropriate thing to call him when talking to you. We can call him Drama Queen... he really doesn't like being called that... oh well.

I know I caused you a lot of mental pain in my attempt to be a parent to you. I did what I thought was right at the time. I have come to realize now that I was a terrible, tyrannical parent to you... maybe tyrant is too strong of a word. But I was a dick either way. In the beginning I was made to believe that your mom was a terrible person and not a good mom, so I felt I needed to compensate for that. Over time I saw that the Drama Queen spoiled you and that you both had each other wrapped around your fingers. So then

I tried to compensate for that. But soon realized that no level of parenting was acceptable to the Drama Queen. I couldn't do anything right no matter how hard I tried. He wouldn't let me have any say in raising you. He feels that a stepparent is not a real parent and should have no tangible part in their step-child's life… unless it was convenient to him. I became resentful of his relationship with you because I loved you so much and felt I couldn't show that on a level that I deemed acceptable.

We grew to dislike each other the more strained our relationship became. I'm sorry for that. During those 7 years of trying to learn how to be a mom and a wife I was also learning first-hand what a narcissist was… though I didn't realize that's what was going on until you were probably 13 or 14 and we didn't see each other very often.

I'm not trying to use this as an excuse for the way I tried to parent you. Knowing what I know now I would do a lot of things differently. I'm just trying to give you some more perspective on the situation.

I'm sorry that I believed the lies I was told. I'm sorry we didn't get along when you were younger. I'm sorry you witnessed some of the fights. Luckily it was just a small portion of the ones that actually occurred. I'm sorry I wasn't there for you for a few years after the divorce. I'm sorry I was such an ass. I'm sorry we live so far away from each other now.

Thank you for teaching me how not to be a mom… in turn you taught me what a good mom should be like. I parent how I do now partly because of you. Thank you for loving me after all the pain I caused you. Thank you for being such an amazing sister to Charlie. Thank you for making me a mom.

I love you mostest bestest.. I win
All My Love
Erin

Dear Rainbow Baby,

My beautiful girl, you are growing so fast. I remember the day you were born like yesterday… you looked at me with those beautiful, too big for your face eyes and I felt I had known you my whole life. I looked at you and I knew what love at first sight was.

I feel I missed so much of your growth focusing on trying to get your brother to be a good person and remain sane during his terrible twos stage. Before that focusing on surviving the relationship with your father, and now trying to fix myself and turn myself into the mother you deserve. I'm sorry. I'm sorry for so much.

I'm sorry that I stayed with your father for so long because of the hurt it caused and because that relationship didn't show you how a healthy relationship is supposed to be. On the other hand, I think if I had left that relationship sooner, I wouldn't have met Dad, so I suppose things happened the way they were meant to.

I'm sorry that your father isn't who I thought he was. And I'm sorry that because of who he is I cannot co-parent with him in the way you deserve.

I'm sorry if your father disappoints you any more than he already has. My fear is that he will disrespect you the way he did your sister, and your sensitive soul will be heartbroken. You are worthy of all the love and respect someone can give to you. I hope that you find someone who is as amazing as Dad is and treats you the way Dad treats me… like a Queen.

I'm sorry I haven't been as understanding as you needed me to be. I am working so hard to be who you need me to be now. I'm so sorry it has taken me so long to realize I needed help before I could be the person you deserve to have as a mother.

I can see you blossoming into an amazing person. I can also see you doubting yourself. I wish you could see yourself through my eyes, for then you would know the extent of how amazing you are. Don't doubt your intelligence, your beauty or any other part of yourself. You are amazing in so many ways. Don't let anyone dull your sparkle or allow them to convince you that you are anything other than awesome. Other people's opinions don't matter. Only accept the best and don't settle for less than wonderful in relationships. I hope that someday you will see how absolutely amazing and beautiful you are.

I love you more than you will ever know.

All My Love
Mommy

Dear My beautiful boy,

You have kept me on my toes from the very beginning. You started life by pooing that black tar poo all over me, but I fell in love with you anyway. You had colic and cried lots in the beginning. Who needs sleep haha. Then we discovered gripe water and it was like a miracle. The fennel calmed your tummy and let you relax a bit.

When you were not quite a year old you got croup for the first time… though at the time I had no idea what croup was. I thought you were going to die on the way to the hospital. Every time you gasped for air my heart broke, I felt like you were slipping away just a little more with every breath. I remember thinking that I had never experienced fear like that. Even with all I had been through before you were born, I still hadn't experienced that level of fear that comes with the thought of losing one of your children.

I lost count of the times we went to the hospital for a nebulizer treatment and steroids over the next year or so. Finally, your doctor told us that it doesn't always help to go to the emergency room and get steroids etc. That sometimes humidifiers and over the counter medication helps just as much. So that's what we did.

Looking back, I think that your breathing problems pushed me onto the path of herbal healing. Without that I wouldn't have had the drive to help people as I do now. Wanting and needing to help your child is like wanting and needing to breathe. It just comes naturally.

Then came the terrible twos. I'm sorry for that ridiculously hard time in our lives and the fact that I wasn't as helpful or as calm as you probably needed me to be.

During this difficult time in your development, I had come to some very harsh realisations about my past and was having a hard time coping with what all that meant. I realise now that it meant I wasn't a very good mom at that strenuous time in your life. I'm sorry.

I'm sorry for not having the patience you deserve. I'm sorry I spent the first five years of your life trying to come to grips with my past and attempting to find myself again. Thankfully I am on the right path now and can be the mom you deserve.

You are extremely intelligent. If you nurture that, there isn't anything you can't do, as long as you remember to be kind and keep your anger in check. Karate or something similar may help you channel that anger to something more structured and positive.

Be respectful and treat others how you want to be treated. Never let someone treat you in a manner less than you deserve. You deserve respect just as everyone else does.

I think it is hard being a boy today because there are so many expectations that contradict each other. Be sensitive. Suck it up and be a man. Don't show your emotions. It's okay to show your emotions. It's difficult to navigate all of this without becoming overwhelmed and confused. I think that if you are respectful and just try to be yourself without trying to fit into anyone's mold of who they think you should be, you will be fine. It is okay to show your emotions, we are all human and emotions are part of who we are and how we interact with each other. Don't be ashamed of them.

You are amazing and beautiful in so many ways. Never stop being you.

I love you to Infinity and Beyond!

All my Love
Mommy

26.

Jade Baxter

To The Ones That Saved Me

To My Beautiful Miracle,

I want to explain everything to you, by the time you read this we will probably have sat down and had the conversation of how you came about. Your biological father and I were not together at the time, but we were still friends. Finding out I was pregnant was a massive shock and I didn't know what to do. You were kept a massive secret on your dad's side until you were born, and I posted a picture of you on social media and there was an identical picture of your sister up too and I had her auntie confront me about your dad. After the conversation back and forth, the name calling our secret was out and we could live in the light instead of the shadows. Then getting into a relationship with the dad of your sister and brothers, things were crazy, but he took you on as his own and raised you.

It's not been an easy ride. A rocky one, with plenty of bumps in the road, from having you and suffering from postnatal depression so bad I missed the first 6 months of your life because I couldn't cope being a mum, then in December 2014 losing the rights as your mum and you and your sister went into foster care. I only got to see you 2 days a week for 2 hours a time. The time this was going on it was incredible hard for me, I fought through the courts and got you and your sister home. I know home life hasn't been easy for us from the breakdown of my relationship with the man who you called dad, and to having siblings move in and out, my mental health and yours being all up in the air but we are together now your brothers, sister, you and mummy.

This is the legacy I want you to remember - no matter how stormy the water is, you can always stride through powerfully like the warrior princess you are. The world can be cruel it's not all roses. Mummy will always be by your side no matter how I feel! YOU MATTER AND COME FIRST!! Don't let your kindness be taken for weakness! Your opinion is so VALID in any situation right or wrong feelings matter! Never hide who you are, embrace it and be authentic and unique. Above anything STAY AWESOME!!!

You will forever be my miracle and my saviour. Each day you grow I couldn't be prouder of you and the young lady you're becoming. With all that has gone on in our lives from heartbreak, separation, loss and more, you amaze me at how you just love and care for everyone putting them before you. You are mummy's best friend.

I love you always and forever

Mummy x

To My Beautiful Toots,

Baby Girl here is my legacy of love letter to you, where do I begin? It has definitely been a rocky road with foster care, separation from your dad, brothers being taken away and brought back as well as you being the wild child.

Times have been hard for sure, trying to understand how your mind works and how you feel at times. By the time you read this I hope we have got the help you need, it's a process but I know you are a special girl. There are times I don't know what to do and I feel like giving up because I can't help you. I know this is not the case.

I know dad leaving is hard, and the inconsistency of contact, but I stopped that for your siblings and your emotional well-being and you children, especially you, need stability. You have so much potential to go far and do well.

One thing I want you to take with you through life is, be who you want to be, you rule your world, remember right from wrong, all feelings are valid.

Love you beautiful

Mummy x

Dear Bub,

Where do I start? At the time I'm writing this letter you are 4 years old; I remember finding out I was pregnant with you. I was over the moon yet terrified.

I'd not had your sisters home long from foster care. I was adapting to being a full-time mum again, then dad coming home to live with us too. Life was chaotic to say the least and then I went for my 20-week scan and was told you were a boy. I cried tears of joy.

I had your name already; I had waited so long to have a son. Your great uncle passed long before you were born and in his remembrance, I named you after him.

I had numerous scans as there were concerns with your heart. You were born with a heart murmur. I saw you briefly then you were rushed off to NICU, it was the scariest time of my whole experience in motherhood not knowing what was going on or being able to hold you. I was taken to the ward surrounded by other mums and their babies, yet I was waiting to hold my baby boy. 6 hours later you were returned to me with a tube in your nose. The doctor confirmed it was a heart murmur, but it should resolve itself, so it was just a waiting game and hospital appointments till we got the all clear that your heart had fixed itself.

The legacy I want to leave you is loyalty, respect, honesty and love. With respect you treat everybody how you want to be treated. This can take you a long way, anybody older than you speak politely to and offer them your seat.

Loyalty is something that comes along with respect and truth, never lie it won't get you far if you do, which is where honesty joins owning the person you become and telling your truth will be your biggest accomplishment in life.

Love is the final part and the hardest. Love comes in various types of ways and can hurt in the worst ways please remember mummy is by your side not matter what... I love you son.

Forever and always

Mummy x

Dear Junior

My last letter to write to my baby boy, you're 3 now and what a 3 years it has been! I feel now we are finally levelling on to the line of stability with bub, your sisters, you and mummy all living together. As you get older there will no doubt be stories flying around but I want you to know, anything I have done has always been in your best interest and for your well-being.

It's been a cycle of emotions with you but seeing the loving, caring, happy little boy you are now makes my heart melt, especially with your cheeky grin. There are no words that can explain the love I have for you and your siblings you all saved mummy in different ways, all my superheroes and my best friends.

Where you will be in years to come? I don't know but whatever the case I will be proud of you.

The legacy I want to leave you is, focus on education remember your feelings are valid. Loyalty, respect and honesty come as one and you should give the same level you want to receive back. Elderly people you come across always be respectful and polite to.

I love you Junior
love Mummy xx

27.

Stina M. Gray

For My Loves, My Reasons, My Life

This is the part of my life that I desperately need to note down, before old age creeps in and the details become foggy. Heaven knows over the years my beautiful mind has been tragically unkind to me and has blocked out many precious memories. Writing helps, as I hope by when you read this, I have had a chance to teach you that.

The world is just coming out of a global pandemic. Basically, a virus took over the world and killed millions of people and made many more really sick. It was like something out of a horror movie! People were walking around in face masks and social distancing. We had three official national lockdowns, like the government actually made it against the law to leave home unless it was essential! Crazy right?

I don't know what your world will be like as each one of you reads this. I hope that I am here for a very long time to witness and explore it with you.

I guess this is the part where I also should probably mention myself. I'm just going to get right to it. Life really kind of sucks right now! Only a few of you will be old enough to remember, thankfully for them, a few of your siblings are oblivious to our family chaos right now. I am waiting to find out if I have a brain tumour! It's about the scariest time, or at least one of the scariest times of my life. Not because I am afraid of dying, the tumour itself is benign, so it won't spread and kill me, but it has the ability to grow and certainly make life difficult... ok and potentially kill me (but that's if it's left untreated!) I am afraid of dying because I don't want to leave you behind. I don't like the idea of any of you growing up without a Mum, which is why some of the darkest hours of my life have been flooded with your light and I have been saved from my tragically beautiful mind. Thank You!

But growing up without a Mum kind of sucks. My Mum gave me away at 13 and it damn near killed me a whole bunch of times throughout my life. It triggered a disorder called Bipolar. I have spent years fighting it and trying desperately to hold it together for you guys. Some days I won, others I had to rest and live to fight another day. There's no shame in that. One of the best things Bipolar did for me was give me the confidence to go out into the world and make a difference. I did all the crazy things that people told me I couldn't.

Growing up I was told I was stupid a lot. It was normally during drunken rage or abusive episodes. The general consensus was that I wouldn't amount to anything. I was just the kid off the council estate that nobody wanted. Even my own Mum gave me away at 13. My Nan raised me and Praise Jesus she did, because she is one of the reasons I have gone on and pushed beyond expectations. She lit a fire in my belly that has burned boldly through anything that ever stood in my way towards Peace. My mental health is the reason I am here writing this Letter in this incredible book. It's the reason I have been able to compile such books filled with incredible authors. You see guys, Mama is kind of a big deal right now! Just in case you thought I was super lame! I rock my pink hair, tattoos and loose lips in a way that has helped hundreds of people publish their stories in my books, thousands of people find a place to safely be themselves and dozens of people (thus far) to remain on this earth. I have literally saved lives from my phone. Talking people away from suicide and being there when people wanted to give up. It sounds big headed when I write it down, but vanity is not something I have ever boasted. I am modest and humble… and a really crap businesswoman! I work too hard for too little. But the mission is to change lives, not grow my bank account.

You see, Just a Mum is one of the legacies I hope to maintain and leave behind for someone to continue my insanely exhausting but worthwhile work, The real legacy is Love. The overwhelming Love for you guys that has saved my life more times than I can tell you. It's pushed me through some really hard times and many days been the only reason I have had to get out of bed. My hope in writing this book, and the others before it, is to give you insight into the world and how you can accomplish anything that you set your mind to. You just have to want it enough and work harder than hard to make it incredible. The Love I have for you guys and the memories we have and will make, is the most powerful thing on this planet! It has survived a pandemic; it has survived a suicidal mind and it has survived every one of our hardships and problems to date.

Love is the most dangerously beautiful thing on Earth. It has the power to build and destroy nations. The power to make or break lives. The power to survive this world long after I have gone. I need you to know that. To know that I love you all fiercely. Equally, in different ways, because you are all different people. I love you with every fibre of my being and I am proud of the people you will become. How do I know that? Because no matter where life takes you, I know that you will find your way! I believe in my heart that for every twist and turn in the road, your journey will be a great one. Each of you. So, I want you all to read these next bits, even though they are addressed individually. There is something in each letter for you all to take away with you, because you are family. Each of you have my blood, my heart and my Soul, entwined eternally with your own. Each of you will be my Legacy of Love. My wish is that you never forget me. That your children's children talk about how epic Nan/Grammie was! (I haven't decided which name I want yet!)

You are my Legacy of Love. My loves, My Reasons, My life.

Dear Kenz,

You are 18 now and 14 weeks away from leaving home and moving to the other side of the country. Oh my god you broke my heart in spectacular ways when you chose Brighton. I was so happy that you chose adventure. That you chose to go out into the world and find yourself. Equally I was devastated that I couldn't just nip round to fist bump you goodnight!

You have had it hard these last few years. Losing Louis was a turning point of your growth. You chose a path afterwards that showed the world that you can be strong, even when your heart is breaking. You get it from your Mama! (Yep, I went there!)

From gangster car music to being an inspiration to your siblings, you have turned out to be an incredible, beautiful woman. I am so proud of your determination. The world will always bring you a shitstorm, but we don't take cover. We dance in through the chaos and weather it like true Gray women. The genetics on that side are fierce and my god are you a pocket rocket. I want to apologise for my Mum's genes. Short in stature, massive boobs (and fod), but you have the Rodgers beauty.

You have way more talent than you know, and I wish you could have more confidence. I wish the world didn't seem such a scary place to just be yourself in. I want to remind you that you came from a strong ass woman and you have already proved that you can handle your own! Go take the world by storm damn it! Go show them that bird who sings and has a thirst for life. Be authentic, always. There is no need to fit in. You were born an individual.

I want you to know that I am proud. That's the most important legacy to leave all of you. I am proud. To be your Mama, to have witnessed your growth and to have helped shape your life in some way.

Never give up. You carry secrets in your heart and sometimes they weigh you down, but never give up. You work hard, you fight hard, and you love harder than anything. Find your reason!

I love you Songbird. More than You know.

All My Love
Mamo xx

Dear Grace,

My funniest child by far! You are hitting that God awful stage of life where everything sucks, the world is unfair, and you just got boobs that you are trying to hide! (Sorry Kid!)

You are a complex character. You come across as hard and not actually caring about much, but you have the most wonderful soul. I see your secret stress, your quiet cries and your worry for everyone (even Ava!). I see how you reach out for hugs from the littles and how badly your heart is breaking at the thought of Kenz leaving you.

You are so beautiful. Not only emotionally but physically too. You are 12 right now and are about the same height as Kenz, you got the Boardman gene there. It's not a bad thing. Being as sporty as you are, it will be a good thing. You love sports. Just like your Dad. You walk around in football shirts and are such a typical teenager. Although, it is pretty awesome to see you in lashes and nails… and joggers! Never change that. Never stop being exactly who you are. Whilst your 'no shits' attitude often gets you into trouble, it a strong thing to take into the world.

I joke with you about not having any interests, but I know that's not true. 'Jeez, I'm 12 Mom!' Yes, you are. You are also mega bossy, but I love it! You have such a strong will and that will be something that takes you far, if you let it. I know when it comes to school, you back away from drama… that makes me proud. School is a hard time in life, but an important one. You don't want to mess it up because some kid got jealous of your popularity. There is great strength in learning to walk away and I hope it's something you continue to grow. I hope that as you grow and go out into the world, you know which the important battles are to choose. That you remember who the heck your Mother is and that she is one of the strongest people you know! That will get you far.

Try to keep an eye on your sisters. You are the strong one. That's not an easy role. Often they will do things to drive you crazy but you have the most incredible kindness in your soul. I am excited to see how you grow. You act like your dad and look like your Mom. That's not a bad thing. We are both awesome people.

You are lucky enough to be surrounded by awesome influences, perhaps not quite old enough yet to appreciate them all, but lucky nevertheless.

I am so proud of who you are. Unique and bold, but also versatile and placid. You are my gorgeous Grace, in every sense of the word. I hope that as you get older you hold onto that and know how much you mean to me. I am keen to see where life takes you. Currently that could be anywhere because the world is still a mystery to you. Wherever it is, go with fun in your heart. Go with laughter and never apologise for being yourself!

I love you Gorgeous Grace. More than You know.

All My Love
Mum, Mom, Mama, Mother!!! Xx

Dear Ava,

Where to begin? You my dear have the biggest heart I have seen. You love so strongly and sometimes it trips you up. You have always been that way. As a toddler you used to follow Grace around and she would brutally forearm you to the face, but you'd get back up and still go back in for a hug! Personal space hasn't always been obvious to you this far, but there is something special about those hugs. Like magic.

You are a beautiful girl. You feel the world deeply. A massive empath. That will serve you well as you grow, if you choose to harness it for a good. Sometimes empaths take on too much of the world's feelings and it can hurt! You have so much love in your heart. I watch as you get frustrated and then get really sad that you got angry or didn't listen. You're 10 right now. You are not supposed to have all the answers at 10! You have never been this age before, and that will be the same when you are 20 or 30. You have never lived that day before so how do you know if you are doing it right or wrong? Just do it. Just live. In whichever way your happy heart desires.

You have a bit of a hippie soul with a science vibe. A rare combination. You want to travel the world and live in a camper van, but you also love maths and science and are super smart! I can see you doing great things as you grow.

You don't have a lot of confidence sometimes. I see that when you get sad about school. By the time you read this you will understand that the mean kids, they never really change, but that's their problem. You will grow into something more spectacular when you dare to dream. When you embrace that difference and be unique.

Ava, your mind is very special, and it fascinates me. You are super clever and MEGA obsessed with

Spiderman. You always have been. You had a toy from my Nan's house when you were young and that's where the interest came from. A legacy of Love for superheroes and all things spectacular.

Try to remember that the world doesn't always feel the same as we do… and that's ok! If we were all the same the world would be super boring. Continue to bake the best cakes and deserts. No seriously, they are awesome! Grow the passion that you have for life.

Never stop being yourself. The world needs people with different opinion and a passion for adventure. I

am so proud of who you are becoming and so excited to see where you will go.

I love you Amazing Ava. More than You Know.

All My Love
Mum xx

Dear Maria,

What can I say? You are six and still have so much of the world to understand yet. You have the most beautiful, long hair and are at the age right now where you love to wind up Nancy! You teach her really cheeky words and how to do Fortnite dances on the trampoline. She loves you. So much.

You have always been a very particular child. You like things done a certain way. Always the first to get out of bed in the morning, never any complaints about having to wake up… but we will check in again when you're Grace's age and see if that's still the same!

Routine has always been a big thing for you. You like to know what's happening and when. It's not a bad thing to hold onto as you grow. Being organised at six years old speaks volumes (hopefully) for the way you will tackle grown up life. I guess only time will tell. Don't be too rigid in your routine. Try to go with the flow sometimes and be spontaneous. It can bring about the most beautiful things.

You currently have a delicate beauty about you. With a little wicked side that likes to be cheeky. You draw me the most awesome pictures and are so thoughtful. You have the most awesome imagination.

Minecraft is your current favourite thing. I remember when you first started playing that, your sisters hated it because all you would do was stand in place and look up to the sky. Looking back, it's quite profound. When you were a baby, I was doing all your firsts whilst doing all Nan's lasts. You only got six months with Grammie, but she was thrilled to give you your first taste of chocolate! She was cheeky like you.

I am excited to watch you grow. To see what things you become interested in, to see how you handle life and to just be as happy as you are when you go and dance in the rain! Your dad thinks I'm crazy for letting you guys do that, but he knows it's good fun. It's also something Papi kept going in me all these years.

Dream often. I'll always meet you in your dreams whenever you want!

I love you Cheeky Maria. More than You Know.

All My Love
Mama xx

Dear Nancy,

There are few words that come close to describing you. As a baby you escaped every restraint and quickly picked up the name Houdini. Right now you are the most wonderfully feral little Boris. You have this wild blonde hair that looks like Boris Johnson (the prime minister that grounded us all during the pandemic!) and Oh My, are you feisty!

Thanks to Ava you have learnt some Spanish and currently your default counting is in Spanish! Not sure how helpful that will be when you start school in September. You are clever. Kenz has taught you a load of things that she shouldn't, Grace has sung frozen songs with you on the trampoline and taught you all kinds of neat tricks. Ava has taught you Spanish and how to love desserts. Maria has driven you crazy and teased you like good sisters should... and Austin, that little dude loves you so much! Even when you kick him in the face! (true story)

I think you might be the child that I get called into school for, purely because your character is so strong! You are like Grace with that. I see all of your siblings in you right now, that's before Papi and I get to instil our infinite wisdom in you. I have no doubts that as you grow your determination and strong will shall grow in harmony.

You are a force of nature that gives some pretty awesome cuddles. You're also a wild ass! Like you genuinely run around without shoes and have spent half your life locked up due to the pandemic. You refused to wear clothes for so long. The world is a magnificent place for you to explore right now (although demanding every toy in Asda yesterday wasn't your finest moment!) Papi has definitely been the Yes man so far. You have been the only child that never slept through until recently, purely because the first instance you cried he would rush upstairs to give you milk… you got used to this and woke every night! Papi's girl.

There is still so much of life for you to explore and like the little genius that you are you will do it in your own way. You are so beautiful and wild. Never change that. Let it be something that drives you and makes you stand out from the world. I hope to be here for many years to watch you take the world by storm. Trust your sisters to guide you. They all have the best qualities and the biggest hearts, with the biggest soft spot for you. You might always be the littlest sister (Papi's short legs!) but you will never be small in a family with so much love to give.

I love You Houdini. More than You Know.

All My Love
Mama xx

Dear Austin,

The Boy. Incubator boy. The one I waited for who died as you were born and then again nine months later decided to almost leave me when you caught meningitis!

You just turned one and it's safe to say that you have given me more medical worries than all your five sisters combined. Even Grace who broke her arm and had to have surgery as a toddler! You my handsome boy have tested our strength and strengthened our capabilities. I never knew I could survive each of your hard times until surviving was the only option. I held you in my arms for 28 hours when you got meningitis. You wouldn't let me put you down. I had to get Papi to bring me pain killers to the hospital. My arm locked.

You were born right at the start of the pandemic. February 2020. Wow, over a year ago. All the shops kept getting closed down and by the time you needed your first pair of shoes, the shoe stores were locked down. You went a year without shoes but had hobbit feet like the rest of us. That was one of my favourite things about the pandemic, not having to wear shoes! Try it. Feet between the grass or the sand. The beach was about the only place we have taken you. That and the most incredibly serene lake in Wales. My favourite places. You have missed out on simple things that the world took for granted. Saying hello to people without a mask covering their face. Going into a store. Oh my god, you truly hate it. The world is beginning to open, and you scream the minute we walk into any kind of store. I've now turned into one of those mums who has to bribe you with Youtube nursery rhymes on my phone as we walk round the store. It worked a treat yesterday as Nancy destroyed the toy shelves.

You are obsessed with Frozen at the moment. If you don't get yourself a girlfriend who looks like Elsa I will be surprised. You sang 'Let it Go' before you talked.

Your sisters adore you and have all been amazing this last year. It's been incredible to take crap family photos where one of you has always looked away or the phone fell right as the timer ran out. You have the cutest smile, and the brightest red hair! Papi had the same hair as you when he was younger but has grown darker as he has aged. He has an epic beard though. You are his double. I don't just mean in looks. You are sweet and jolly. Ha, that always reminds me of chubby, but it's not what I mean! You have an awesome smile and beautiful eyes.

The world is yet to bring you memories and experiences. I hope they are joyous and filled with wonderment. You are a strong boy and have overcome so much in your one short year. Long may that strength continue. You have to keep an eye those emotional sisters of yours but know and understand that men get emotional too. As much as you will watch out for them, let them watch out for you also.

I love You Little Lion Man. More than You know.

All My Love
Mom xx

So, there you have it guys, I don't plan on leaving this world soon. I still have too much work to be done. There's an entire world to explore and many, many lives to change. Each of you have taught me something new about myself and our world. You have given me strength in different ways, and you have all saved my life. Without even knowing it.

I have times when I am scared, times when I fight strong but feel weak. We all do… and that's ok. If I can give you anything it's those three words. 'And that's OK!' Those three words give you the power to accept yourself in whatever situation you find yourself in. They give permission to the feelings you have and bring Peace when the world's expectations don't quite align with your capabilities at the time.

My legacy is not this book or the network of women, My Legacy is You. Six beautiful children, who will make pancakes like Nan did, who will bake cookies and watch movies on a Sunday night. Legacies that will sit around the table for family dinners and play who can be the quietest the longest (the most difficult game in the world for you guys!) But you are all strong willed and wonderful. You have changed my life and taken it to a place where I can make a difference.

Work hard but love harder. Never get stuck with pride over peace. Be humble. Grateful. Kind. Focus on the impact you can have on the world, not on the approval of others.

Dance in the rain and wrestle in the front room. Take long drives to beautiful places and know the strength in the blossom trees. They withstand each cold winter, strong but bare. Not always the most beautiful or bright trees, but nevertheless, strong enough to weather the storm. Then each year they bloom. Blossom beautifully. Time and again, no matter how harsh the winter was, their incredible beauty comes back better than before as they grow!

Blossom into the Badass Humans that came from a Warrior Queen. Be yourself. Always. There is no person better than you. There are only people. Beautifully unique, finding their own way in this crazy world.

Peace and Love xx

Afterthought

So, there you have it! A Legacy of Love immortalised on the world wide web and in print for ever and ever. It feels pretty good to get to the end of a book, especially as a Mum who struggles to pee in peace, let alone read epic letters from epic women!! But it feels good. I think if there's one thing that we can learn from this book it's that time is the most precious gift aside of our children. Time can be crafted to move mountains and survive oceans. It's something we too often take for granted.

The world is not promised. A year of covid lockdowns and uncertainty should be testament to that. Maslow would be raging if he saw the basic needs of his hierarchy demolished by a deadly virus! We were all lost for a little while. Questioning our place in society, the state of our health and the future of the world as we knew it. One thing that stood out as it stood still… time. If last year taught us anything it was that slowing life down to appreciate the most basic of things was a great gift. A hug. Taken away for so long, but one of the things we craved and sadly in some cases, will continue to do so, with only memories remaining. Shaking hands or standing next to strangers on the met. Everything now sits 6 foot apart and is wiped down if you even look in its direction.

But this is history. We get to tell our stories of toilet roll and pasta scavenges. Home schooling and doorstep rounds of applause. We get to pass on a Legacy of survival when so many didn't get the chance. We get to honour the fallen and celebrate the survivors. We get to live again. Fresh start. From the very moment you put down this book. You get to make that choice. To do something different in your world. To focus on impact rather than waste a lifetime looking for approval. You get to choose the Legacy of Love that you leave from this day forth.

Make it Magic. Dream big and never stop at the stars.

Stina M. Gray – Just a Mum, Warrior and Queen

Just a Mum – Warrior and Queen can be found on both Instagram and Facebook where we continue to support, showcase and empower individuals around the world.

All Materials and Services can be found at:
www.warriorandqueen.com

Warrior and Queen are a Counsellor lead Empowerment movement providing Training Courses, Webinars, International Public Speaking, 1-1 Sessions, Reading Materials and Online Support to Communities around the world.

Founder – Stina M. Gray
Public Speaker, Counsellor and Author
Badass Mother of Six Children
Just a Mum – Warrior and Queen

"Focus on Impact – Not on Approval"

You're Never Just a Mum

Printed in Great Britain
by Amazon

61768900R00142